Children and Welfare Reform: Highlights from Recent Research

Ann Collins
Stephanie Jones
Heather Bloom

The **NATIONAL CENTER FOR CHILDREN IN POVERTY** (NCCP) was established in 1989 at the School of Public Health, Columbia University. Its mission is to identify and promote strategies that reduce the number of young children living in poverty in the United States, and that improve the life chances of the millions of children under six who are growing up poor.

The Center:

- Alerts the public to demographic statistics about child poverty and to the scientific research on the serious impact of poverty on young children, their families, and their communities.

- Designs and conducts field-based studies to identify programs, policies, and practices that work best for young children and their families living in poverty.

- Disseminates information about early childhood care and education, child health, and family and community support to government officials, private organizations, and child advocates, and provides a state and local perspective on relevant national issues.

- Brings together public and private groups to assess the efficacy of current and potential strategies to lower the young child poverty rate and to improve the well-being of young children in poverty, their families, and their communities.

- Challenges policymakers and opinion leaders to help ameliorate the adverse consequences of poverty on young children.

Children and Welfare Reform: Highlights from Recent Research, by Ann Collins, Stephanie Jones, and Heather Bloom. Ann Collins is program associate for early childhood care and education, NCCP; Stephanie Jones is research associate, NCCP; and Heather Bloom is a graduate of Columbia University School of International and Public Affairs.

The Center appreciates the generous support from the Annie E. Casey Foundation that funded this publication. The Center also gratefully acknowledges the Ford Foundation and the Carnegie Corporation of New York for their core support of the Center and its publications program.

```
                    HV 699 .C65 1996
                    Collins, Ann.
                    Children and welfare reform

                    occOR Sep-09-1998 16:50
```

Copies of this research highlights are available @ $10.00 prepaid by writing the National Center for Children in Poverty, Columbia University School of Public Health, 154 Haven Avenue, New York, NY 10032; Tel: (212) 927-8793; Fax: (212) 927-9162; E-mail: ejs22@columbia.edu; WWW: http://cpmcnet.columbia/dept/nccp/.

© 1996 by the National Center for Children in Poverty.

ISBN 0-926582-17-8

CONTENTS

INTRODUCTION 5

DEVELOPMENTAL RISKS FOR CHILDREN IN POVERTY 14

The Life Circumstances and Development of Children in Welfare Families: A Profile Based on National Survey Data. Nicholas Zill, Kristin A. Moore, Ellen Wolpow Smith, Thomas Stief, and Mary Jo Coiro 14

Economic Deprivation and Early Childhood Development. Greg J. Duncan, Jeanne Brooks-Gunn, and Pamela Kato Klebanov 15

Succeeding Generations: On the Effects of Investments in Children. Robert Haveman and Barbara Wolfe 17

The Strain of Living Poor: Parenting, Social Support, and Child Mental Health. Vonnie C. McLoyd and Leon Wilson 18

Growing Up with a Single Parent: What Hurts, What Helps. Sara McLanahan and Gary Sandefur 19

PROFILES OF ADULTS ON AFDC 21

Welfare That Works: The Working Lives of AFDC Recipients. Roberta Spalter-Roth, Beverly Burr, Heidi Hartmann, and Lois Shaw 21

The Health, Earnings Capacity, and Poverty of Single-Mother Families. Barbara L. Wolfe and Steven Hill 22

Poverty and Women's Mental Health. Deborah Belle 23

ECONOMIC ISSUES FOR FAMILIES LEAVING WELFARE FOR WORK 24

Finding Work in the Inner City: How Hard is it Now? How Hard Will it be for AFDC Recipients? Katherine Newman and Chauncy Lennon 24

When Welfare Ends: Subsistence Strategies of Former GA Recipients, Final Report of the General Assistance Project. Sandra Danziger and Sherrie Kossoudji 26

PROGRAM STRATEGIES AND THEIR IMPLICATIONS FOR CHILDREN 28

Programs to Enhance the Self-Sufficiency of Welfare Families: Pathways of Effects on Young Children. Martha Zaslow, Kristin Moore, Mary Jo Coiro, and Donna Ruane Morrison 28

Poor Children and Welfare Reform. Olivia Golden 29

Two Generation Programs for Families in Poverty: A New Intervention Strategy. Sheila Smith 31

Bridging the Worlds of Head Start and Welfare-to-Work: Building a Two-Generation Self-Sufficiency Program from the Ground Up, Revised Edition. Toby Herr and Robert Halpern, with Ria Majeske 32

Changing What Counts: Rethinking the Journey Out of Welfare. Toby Herr, Robert Halpern, with Aimee Conrad 34

Five Years After: The Long-Term Effects of Welfare-to-Work Programs. Daniel Friedlander and Gary Burtless 35

Welfare Realities: From Rhetoric to Reform. Mary Jo Bane and David T. Ellwood 36

Welfare Spending in State Budgets. Sarah Ritchie 37

CHILD CARE 39

Caring for Children at the Poverty Line. Sandra L. Hofferth 39

Child Care and AFDC Recipients in Illinois: Patterns, Problems and Needs.
Gary L. Siegel, and L. Anthony Loman 40

GAIN Family Life and Child Care Study Technical Report. Marcia K. Meyers, Neil Gilbert, and Jill Duerr-Berrick 42

Child Day Care in Welfare Reform: Are We Targeting Too Narrowly? Marcia K. Meyers 44

Cost, Quality, and Child Outcomes in Child Care Centers. Executive Summary.
Suzanne Helburn, Mary L. Culkin, John Morris, Naci Mocan, Carollee Howes, Leslie Phillipsen, Donna Bryant, Richard Clifford, Debby Cryer, Ellen Peisner-Feinberg, Margaret Burchinal, Sharon Lynn Kagan, and Jean Rustici 45

Early Childhood Centers: Services to Prepare Children for School Often Limited.
Report to the Ranking Minority Member, Senate Subcommittee on Children and Families, Committee on Labor and Human Resources, U.S. Senate 46

The Florida Child Care Quality Improvement Study, Interim Report. Carollee Howes, Ellen Smith, and Ellen Galinsky 49

The Study of Children in Family Child Care and Relative Care: Highlights of Findings.
Ellen Galinsky, Carollee Howes, Susan Kontos, and Marybeth Shinn 50

CHILD HEALTH

Child Health and Poor Children. Sara Rosenbaum 52

State Initiatives to Cover Uninsured Children. Ian T. Hill, Lawrence Bartlett, and Molly B. Brostrom 53

State Initiatives to Provide Medical Coverage for Uninsured Children.
Christopher DeGraw, Jane Park, and Julie A. Hudman 55

FAMILIES WITH TEENAGE PARENTS: STRATEGIES TO INCREASE THEIR LIFE CHANCES 57

New Chance: Interim Findings on a Comprehensive Program for Disadvantaged Young Mothers and Their Children. Janet C. Quint, Denise F. Polit, Hans Bos, and George Cave 57

The Challenges of Serving Teenage Mothers: Lessons From Project Redirection.
Denise Polit, Janet Quint, and James Riccio 58

The Educational Effects of LEAP and Enhanced Services in Cleveland: Ohio's Learning, Earning, and Parenting Program for Teenage Parents on Welfare. David Long, Robert G. Wood, Hilary Kopp, and Rebecca Fisher 60

The Effects of Welfare Reform on Teenage Parents and Their Children. J. Lawrence Aber, Jeanne Brooks-Gunn, and Rebecca Maynard 61

Welfare Dependency: Coordinated Community Efforts Can Better Serve Young At-Risk Teen Girls. Report to the Ranking Minority Member, Committee on Finance, U.S. Senate 63

GLOSSARY 66

INTRODUCTION

NATIONAL CONTEXT

The mid-1990s mark an era of experimentation in welfare initiatives. Even prior to federal welfare reform deliberations during 1995 and 1996, many states had moved forward with welfare experiments. As of February 1996, 38 states had received waivers from federal law to implement new strategies. The majority of these efforts had at least one of three principal goals: (1) to move adults receiving Aid to Families with Dependent Children (AFDC) into the workforce; (2) to decrease the number of new births to mothers on AFDC (or at risk of needing AFDC); and (3) to decrease the cost of welfare programs.

Although these goals do not relate directly to children in families on AFDC, any effort to meet these goals would have a significant impact on children's lives. Two-thirds of AFDC recipients are children, and in sheer numbers alone, children on AFDC are likely to be the largest population group to feel the effects of welfare reforms.

In this volume, *Children and Welfare Reform: Highlights from Recent Research*, the National Center for Children in Poverty summarizes what is known about children and welfare reform. To develop the publication, project staff looked for research studies on children and parents in poverty, studies of program models likely to have direct implications for children, and outcome evaluations of welfare-to-work programs that show how some of the programs affect children.

We sought research that would illuminate at least one of the three major ways that welfare reform could affect children's growth and development: (1) by affecting family income; (2) by affecting the levels of stress on adults receiving AFDC and their parenting styles; or (3) by influencing the access to and the quality of services that children receive.

The resulting 34 reports, articles, and studies cover the following seven categories:
- Developmental Risks for Children in Poverty
- Profiles of Adults on AFDC
- Economic Issues for Families Leaving Welfare for Work
- Program Strategies and Their Implications for Children
- Child Care
- Child Health
- Families with Teenage Parents: Strategies to Increase Their Life Chances

The summaries of these reports paint a remarkably consistent picture of families and children in poverty and of the capacity of interventions to either lift families out of poverty or to provide enhanced services for children. However, the picture is based on a series of safety net programs that are likely to change significantly, perhaps in the near future. In addition to considering AFDC, many of the studies took into account other programs targeted to low-income families, including Medicaid, the Earned Income Tax Credit (EITC), Supplemental Security Income

(SSI), the Dependent Care Tax Credit (DCTC), child care subsidies, prekindergarten programs, and education and training programs for low-income adults.

Lessons learned in the seven categories are summarized below.

DEVELOPMENTAL RISKS FOR CHILDREN IN POVERTY

In recent years, large data sets such as data from the decennial Census or the Current Population Survey (CPS) have enabled researchers to develop "snap shots" of children and families in poverty. Several longitudinal data sets are now also available that contain survey information gathered at regular intervals from the same households, such as the Panel Study of Income Dynamics (PSID) and the National Longitudinal Survey of Youth (NLSY). These data sets, along with rich information gathered from participants in programs designed to reduce the incidence of poverty or deflect its damaging effects, offer glimpses of the interrelations among poverty, parenting, interventions, and children's development. The glossary of this report describes the data sets used by the researchers.

The findings from several of these key studies are featured on pages 14–20. All the studies examined in this section found that family economic status, and the degree of persistence of poverty, were powerful predictors of children's current status (see Duncan, Brooks-Gunn, and Klebanov, 1991) and later success (see Haveman and Wolfe, 1994). For instance, the work of Zill, Moore, Smith, Stief, and Coiro (1991) helps us understand the similarities between children on AFDC and other low-income children, as compared to nonpoor children. Their findings indicate that it is *poverty* that affects children's well-being, not whether a family's primary source of income is AFDC or wages. Family- and individual-related factors, such as whether families were headed by single mothers, the level of maternal education, the number of years mothers received welfare, and low birthweights, were also strongly associated with later success (see Haveman and Wolfe, 1994).

The research in this section also indicates that one major way poverty affects children's growth and development is through its effect on parents. Work by McLoyd and Wilson (1991) describes a link between economic hardship and mothers' psychological distress and mental health status. This research found that economic hardship was not directly related to the level of children's stress, but was related to mothers' psychological functioning, which in turn was related to stress levels for children.

All of these factors have serious consequences for children, ranging from health problems (Zill et al., 1991); lower IQs (Duncan et al., 1991); more behavioral problems (Duncan et al., 1991); less years of education and poorer performance in school (Zill et al., 1991; Haveman and Wolfe, 1994); less likelihood of completing high school (McLanahan and Sandefur, 1994; Haveman and Wolfe, 1994), lower economic productivity for young people in their mid-twenties (Haveman and Wolfe, 1994); and greater chances for girls to become single mothers (McLanahan and Sandefur, 1994; Haveman and Wolfe, 1994).

The research in this section indicates that the effects of current welfare reform activities on family income (and other factors related to family income, such as mothers' education level) may have important consequences for children. The potential effects may go beyond issues related directly to material deprivation (such as not having enough food, or living in poor neighborhoods) to the quality of parenting that children receive.

PROFILES OF ADULTS ON AFDC

An understanding of some key characteristics of adult AFDC recipients—who are most often single mothers—is important for developing expectations about the capacity of these women to fulfill the dual roles of wage earners and parents.* Many studies over the last few years have examined these issues. However, only three were highlighted here. In the first, Spalter-Roth, Burr, Hartmann, and Shaw's (1995) analysis of Survey of Income and Program Participation (SIPP) data shows that the majority of women receiving AFDC had participated in the labor force over the prior two-year period or had spent substantial time seeking jobs. The study also shows that a community's economic environment, and a woman's education, job history, and health status are closely tied with the probability that a woman will rely on AFDC. These characteristics include not being disabled, living in states with low rates of unemployment, having less need for expensive child care (e.g., for infants and toddlers), and having more education, job training, and prior work experience.

Wolfe and Hill (1993) show that 7 percent of women on AFDC have health problems that greatly reduce their earning capacity. These researchers also demonstrate the economic importance of good health. The study showed that 100 percent of families headed by single women in poor or fair health, a significant proportion of whom are receiving at least one nonwage source of income (such as AFDC, SSI, disability insurance, or child support payments) *would* be poor if they were forced to rely solely on the mothers' earning capacity for income. Finally, Belle (1990) summarizes research on the effects of poverty on women's mental health, citing a number of studies that show the links between economic hardship and stress, depression, and other mental health conditions.

Although these three analyses are by no means representative, they highlight the fact that families headed by single parents on AFDC are similar to other families in poverty in several ways. Many parents on AFDC use cash benefits as their income source between jobs. Welfare thus serves as an employment-related safety net in much the same way that other workers, who have firmer ties with the labor force, use unemployment insurance. The studies also examine the ways in which health and mental health status relate to poverty status, and how this again relates to mothers' parenting and wage earning capacities. All three studies are important for developing reasonable expectations about welfare-to-work programs and designing interventions that get to the core causes of single-mother families living in poverty.

---

* We consider issues related to teenage parents on AFDC separately.

Economic Issues for Families Leaving Welfare for Work

Current policy efforts to move women into *any* employment, regardless of income, and the fact that most women who move from welfare to work obtain low-wage jobs (with or without policy interventions), underscore the importance of developing a better understanding of low-wage employment and families' long-term economic prospects. Because this is such a critical issue, we focus on two studies that provide additional information to that summarized in the previous section on AFDC.

In the first study, Newman and Lennon (1995) examine minority workers' employment opportunities in the low-wage fast-food industry in Harlem, where the average fast-food job wage was $4.59 an hour. The study found that for each fast-food job there were 14 applicants, and that job seekers had applied previously for four or five other jobs before applying for the fast-food job. New hires were disproportionately older than 20, with the largest number of workers aged 25 or over. Employers showed a preference for applicants who were not African American, even in central Harlem, where the majority of the population is African American.

The second study in this section (Danziger and Kossoudji, 1995) looks at single individuals who had formerly received cash assistance through Michigan's General Assistance (GA) program. This is a different population from AFDC recipients. Two years after the GA program terminated in 1991, the researchers interviewed 426 former GA recipients about health, program assistance, employment, housing, family, and emotional well-being. The researchers found that the former GA recipients, even after adding up all cash resources, were living on the edge of subsistence. Economic outcomes varied significantly by age and health status. More than half of the younger, more healthy respondents worked in a formal job in the second post-GA year, but fewer than one in three older healthy respondents, and only one in eight older chronically ill respondents, were employed during the same period.

The two studies show the need for reasonable expectations about the results of welfare reform practices that provide little to no support (from more intensive education to less intensive job placement) to less educated recipients, who may also have additional barriers to employment. These studies indicate that it should be expected that at least some AFDC recipients will be unable to find and maintain employment. Even when employment is possible, it is likely that a proportion of the current AFDC population would suffer losses in family income after going to work, especially if income supplements (e.g., partial AFDC benefits, child care subsidies, Medicaid, EITC) were unavailable to them.

Program Strategies and Their Implications for Children

In the mid-1980s, states and communities launched several new types of welfare-to-work programs that ultimately led to the development of the Family Support Act (FSA) of 1988. Many aspects of these programs and the states' implementation of the FSA have been evaluated. Research includes formal outcome evaluations to identify the effects of these programs (often measuring economic outcomes for families and cost savings for states), implementation issues, and promising program models. However, very few studies to date look specifically at the effects of such programs on children's growth and development. In this area, there is much to be learned.

Although there were more limited studies to draw from, this section summarizes studies that provide some insights into how adult-focused program strategies can affect children. Zaslow, Moore, Coiro, and Morrison (1994) reviewed evidence from seven welfare-to-work programs, some of which focused on teenage parents. These authors found that the studies revealed some moderate impacts on family income, parenting, and children's services. These welfare reform activities led to some gains in earnings and reductions in AFDC receipt, and, where measured, gains in educational attainment. Those programs that included a parenting component resulted in increased levels of participation in parenting-related activities; however, the measurable results were moderate. Also, the adequacy of child care had a significant impact on whether parents continued to make progress in moving from welfare to work. (The studies did not measure how the adequacy of child care affected children's growth and development.)

Friedlander and Burtless (1995) also provide important information about the long-term economic impacts of welfare-to-work programs. They summarize the five-year impacts of four welfare-to-work programs evaluated by the Manpower Demonstration Research Corporation (MDRC), learning that the five-year earnings of program participants greatly exceeded the original two-year findings on earnings. However, because AFDC benefit levels are reduced for individuals whose incomes increase, the overall financial position of enrollees improved only in two of the four programs. Bane and Ellwood (1994) discuss the patterns of welfare use, and find that education and previous work experience are powerful predictors of leaving AFDC and obtaining moderate earnings increases.

Four other publications summarized in this section (Golden, 1992; Smith, 1995; Herr, Halpern, and Majeske, 1994; Herr, Halpern, and Conrad, 1991) discuss different program strategies that can potentially have an impact on children. Herr et al. (1991 and 1994) reports on Project Match, an inner-city Chicago program that works with AFDC recipients living in the Cabrini-Green housing development, a model in which small steps (which include increasing parental responsibility) are like rungs on a ladder. The steps ultimately can lead to economic self-sufficiency. In one study (Herr et al., 1994), the authors present a model where parental participation in Head Start programs can lead to greater employment activities. Golden (1992) and Smith (1995) both discuss models of programs that have a dual focus on adults and on children in low-income families. Golden (1992) discusses the importance of case management in welfare programs, and Smith's (1995) compilation describes a range of "two-generational" programs that may ultimately increase parents' ability to increase their earning capacities—while also providing high-quality early childhood services to children.

The final publication in this section (Ritchie, 1993) assesses the capacities of state funding sources to pay for welfare and related programs. The assessment found that although general welfare was a small and declining proportion of state budgets, welfare spending varied widely across states, with the affluence of a state having a major impact on the generosity of its program.

Taken together, the studies, evaluations, and model program descriptions in this section are instructive about potential welfare reform program strategies and show the need for more child-focused evaluations. They show that a few states and communities have launched thoughtful welfare reform activities that—even when focused primarily on adult-related goals—pay mind to the needs of individual families, and especially to the needs of children. However, we have little evaluation information available about their impacts on children.

We know the most about the income effects of straightforward, adult-focused welfare-to-work strategies. Research indicates that the most successful programs to date result in only moderate gains in family income. Such welfare-to-work programs logically lead to families using additional child care, but little to nothing is known about its quality or its effects on children. It is clear that additional information is needed in this critical area.

CHILD CARE

All of the welfare-to-work strategies studied point to the importance of adequate child care if parents are to be successful in working or preparing for work. Clearly, child care is also important for children's growth and development. This section summarizes some important new research in this area. Helburn et al. (1995) and Galinsky, Howes, Kontos, and Shinn (1994) each have completed research that looks at the quality of care in early childhood settings. The former focuses on center-based care, and the latter on family child care. These studies reported that the great majority of child care ranged between adequate or mediocre quality (neither growth-enhancing nor growth-harming), and poor quality (growth-harming). The quality of care for infants and toddlers found in centers was of particular concern.

Both studies found evidence of direct ties between child care quality and children's growth and development. In the Helburn et al. (1995) study, children from low-income families were especially affected by both good and poor quality care. In another study, Howes, Smith, and Galinsky (1995) provide an example of how increased regulation can positively affect children's growth and development. The U.S. General Accounting Office (1995) report on early childhood centers showed the importance of developmentally appropriate, high-quality, early childhood services to prepare children for school; however, it recognizes that most disadvantaged children do not attend early childhood centers.

Another group of studies tracks the child care experiences of low-income families, particularly those who are working and receiving AFDC, or those at risk of needing it. Siegel and Loman (1991) showed that most Illinois families using AFDC or leaving AFDC for work relied heavily on informal care. Only 25 percent of those in the Siegel and Loman (1991) study who wanted center-based care actually used this type of care. The researchers also showed that child care problems prevented AFDC recipients from working or going to school. Similarly, Meyers (1995), after tracking GAIN program participants over a two-year period, demonstrated that the adequacy of child care was a predictor of parents' success in the program. Other work by Meyers, Gilbert, and Duerr-Berrick (1992) indicated that despite their need for child care subsidies, many families were not aware that subsidies were available. Finally, Hofferth (1995) compared child care needs, constraints, and uses of subsidies and tax credits between working poor, working-class, and middle-class families, indicating that working poor families faced several significant constraints to using child care programs. These include work schedules, a lack of affordable options, and limited availability of government assistance.

Taken together, this recent research points to some great concerns about difficult issues related to welfare reform activities and child care. Many of the evaluations of welfare-to-work programs and analyses of families' barriers to work cited in this report point to the importance of child care for adults to be successful in their efforts to work and/or prepare for work. Child care has a clear potential to affect children as well. Welfare reform efforts that result in more children receiving poor quality care will be harmful to the growth and development of children.

However, child care quality issues, while felt most intensely by some low-income families, are systemic to the child care market in the U.S. Instead of evaluating ways to increase the quality of care for the specific, narrow population of low-income families reliant on welfare, recent research has evaluated the efficacy of efforts to improve the quality of "formal" child care programs across incomes—child care centers and family child care homes that operate as small businesses—and has shown promising results. However, studies do not provide insights into ways to improve the quality of an important segment of the child care market: care provided by families, friends, and neighbors. It is likely that many families moving from welfare to work will need and use such care because of their preferences, nontraditional work hours, and the lack of other feasible options.

CHILD HEALTH

Access to primary and preventive care is important for low-income families. Rosenbaum (1992) summarizes research on basic indicators of child health and shows that poor progress in improving child health can be seen in nearly every basic child health indicator. She argues that health insurance status is closely linked to family income, and that at the time of writing the article, modest improvements in publicly-funded health insurance like Medicaid were inadequate to offset the decline in employer coverage.

The Zill et al. (1991) study (in the first section) indicates that children on AFDC, through their automatic eligibility to the Medicaid program, are better-off than other poor children with respect to health insurance coverage and access to medical care. Since families moving from AFDC to work often get jobs that lack benefits (and concurrently lose their entitlement to Medicaid unless states specify otherwise under current law), child health insurance is a significant issue. For this reason, two additional articles (Hill, Bartlett, and Brostrom, 1993; Degraw, Park, and Hudman, 1995) are summarized that describe efforts to expand child health insurance coverage to families with somewhat higher incomes than those on AFDC.

FAMILIES WITH TEENAGE PARENTS: STRATEGIES TO INCREASE THEIR LIFE CHANCES

This section summarizes several evaluations of programs designed to enhance the life skills of low-income teenage parents, including the New Chance program, Project Redirection, Learning Earning and Parenting (LEAP), and the Teenage Parent Demonstration program. These studies varied in the extent to which they attempted to measure issues directly related to developmental outcomes for children. The findings from these studies show that teenage parent programs result in moderate to mixed success in helping adolescents take steps toward self-sufficiency and ensuring that children of teenage parents get the parenting and services needed for healthy growth and development. (Quint, Polit, Bos, and Cave, 1994; Aber, Brooks-Gunn, and Maynard, 1995).

Finally, the U.S. General Accounting Office (1995) report in this section describes the health and well-being of young, at-risk teenage girls and their families, and the conditions of urban neighborhoods where they live. It also offers insights about the successes and failures of pregnancy prevention programs and programs for teenage parents. The report shows that poverty, substance abuse, physical and sexual abuse, and neglect have left teenage girls isolated and vulnerable. These girls are at risk for multiple problems. The report argues that at-risk teenage girls could be better served if intervention approaches included early identification and treatment, long-term program commitment, and greater community involvement.

This section was included in *Children and Welfare Reform: Highlights from Recent Research* because women who become mothers as adolescents are at risk of long-term welfare recipiency (Bane and Ellwood, 1994) and they have some very specific needs. The studies here provide information about some promising effects of programs for adolescent parents. However, they also highlight the fact that the deep and complex problems faced by young parents do not lend themselves well to simple, standard program solutions. Addressing certain core issues that lead to adolescent parenting and other bad outcomes for adolescents may be a way to bring down the teen pregnancy rate.

IMPLICATIONS FOR A CHILDREN'S PERSPECTIVE ON WELFARE REFORM

The rich research summarized in this report leads to several conclusions about the implications of welfare reform for family income, parenting and parental stress, and children's access to services. Some fundamental implications are described below.

- **Family income**

Research to date suggests it is poverty and not whether families receive cash assistance that impedes children's growth and development. It does so in ways that significantly affect children's future life chances. *Therefore, it is unlikely that welfare reforms that leave families in poverty will improve children's prospects. Reforms that cause deeper and more persistent poverty than heretofore will negatively affect children's growth and development. If income rises significantly for some families as a result of welfare reform, there can be improvements for the healthy growth and development of children.*

Many of the interventions evaluated to date have had, at best, only moderate effects on raising family income. For instance, Friedlander and Burtless (1995) noted that long-term evaluations of welfare reform strategies show that family income has changed little as a result of welfare-to-work programs. There is very little knowledge available about some of the policy interventions now under discussion.

- **Parenting**

Research shows that one way poverty affects children is by influencing the behavior of their parents. Parents struggling with poverty are less likely to have the necessary psychological resources that are needed to be good parents. They also may be stressed or withdrawn, angry or punitive, or anxious and erratic. *Welfare reforms that increase parental stress may have negative consequences for children. On the other hand, policies that contribute to experiences and life circumstances that strengthen parents' psychological resources could have positive consequences.*

Current research makes it unclear how newly designed welfare programs will affect parents. We have very little research available to us on this point. Those few studies of welfare-to-work programs completed to date—ones that attempt to measure at least some effects in parenting styles—have found few measurable effects.

- **Children's services**

Poverty limits access to high-quality children's services, including child care, early education experiences, and health care. Research shows that poor quality child care can impede children's growth and development, while high-quality care promotes healthy growth and development. These effects are largest for low-income children. In addition, research confirms the importance of access to health insurance and primary care for children. *Welfare reforms that put children in low-quality child care and limit their access to health care can significantly harm children. On the other hand, welfare reform that enables families to obtain high-quality child care and access to health care can have positive consequences for children.*

Despite the research completed on these important issues, unanswered questions remain. Additional research and evaluations are needed to fully understand the pathways by which new welfare reforms will affect children. In the meantime, information already available underscores the need for caution when developing and implementing interventions. How much to expect from any single intervention should be carefully considered and close attention should be given to the many complex issues that surround children and families receiving welfare.

DEVELOPMENTAL RISKS FOR CHILDREN IN POVERTY

"Family economic status and the degree of poverty persistence were powerful predictors of children's cognitive development, depression, and aggression."

—See *Economic Deprivation and Early Childhood* annotation.

The Life Circumstances and Development of Children in Welfare Families: A Profile Based on National Survey Data. (1991). Nicholas Zill, Kristin A. Moore, Ellen Wolpow Smith, Thomas Stief, and Mary Jo Coiro. Child Trends, Inc., 4301 Connecticut Avenue, NW, Suite 100, Washington, DC 20008. (202) 362-5580/Fax (202) 362-5533. (60 pp.; $14.50).

Implications for a children's perspective

The report describes the circumstances of children in families who receive Aid to Families with Dependent Children (AFDC), and compares them with two large and nationally representative samples of U.S. families with children. The authors compare children on AFDC to other poor children and to nonpoor children in terms of several measurements that relate to the growth and development of children.

Study design

The study used two national samples of children who receive welfare benefits, the National Health Interview Survey, Child Health Supplement (NHIS-CHS) and the National Longitudinal Survey of Youth (NLSY), both to describe the circumstances of children in families on welfare and to determine whether their problems are closely associated with welfare dependency or other issues related to poverty. The research also describes the home environments of these children and attempts to determine the effects of Medicaid and other welfare-linked programs. (Please see acronyms in the glossary for a more complete description of data sets.)

Relevant findings

- Poor children from families not on welfare had equivalent levels of health and behavior problems, and nearly as severe learning problems as those from AFDC families. This may mean that if families move from "welfare poor" to "working poor," the overall developmental status and future life chances of children will not necessarily improve. Low parent education, poverty, and family turmoil are detrimental to children's development, regardless of the source of family income or the predominant family structure.

- **Children in AFDC families had slightly more severe learning problems than those in other poor families.** For example, 60 percent of AFDC children, 55 percent of non-AFDC poor children, and 41 percent of nonpoor children performed in the bottom half of their class at school. Likewise, 60 percent of AFDC children, 47 percent of non-AFDC poor children, and 27 percent of nonpoor children scored below the 30th percentile on vocabulary tests.

However, when controlling for differences in parent education, racial and ethnic composition, family structure, and other factors, the level of differences between poor AFDC children and other poor children was reduced.

- **Poor children (AFDC and non-AFDC) were significantly less healthy, more than twice as likely to fail in school, and more likely to present serious conduct and discipline problems to teachers and parents than were nonpoor children.** Thirty-two percent of poor children (AFDC and non-AFDC) were in excellent health with no activity limitations or developmental problems, as compared to 48 percent of nonpoor children.

- **Only one-third of preschool children from poor families (AFDC and non-AFDC) received the intellectual stimulation and emotional support from their parents that children in nonpoor families received.** Two-thirds of three- to five-year-olds whose families received AFDC were growing up in "below average" home environments in terms of stimulation and support, and nearly one-quarter were receiving clearly "deficient" care. There was a similar breakdown for poor, non-AFDC families.

- **Health-related factors in the home environments of many poor children's families (AFDC and non-AFDC) were less satisfactory than those in nonpoor families.** These factors include parental smoking, children's seat belt use habits, and regular and reasonable children's bedtimes.

- **Children receiving AFDC were substantially better-off than other poor children with respect to health insurance coverage and access to medical care.** Poor children in non-AFDC families were six times more likely to lack health insurance coverage, and were twice as likely to lack a source of routine medical care. This finding reinforced concerns about the possible negative effects on children who lose Medicaid benefits as parents move from AFDC dependency to precarious self-sufficiency.

Economic Deprivation and Early Childhood Development. (1994). Greg J. Duncan, Jeanne Brooks-Gunn, and Pamela Kato Klebanov. *Child Development*, 65 (2), pp. 296–318. (Special issue: Children and Poverty. Aletha C. Huston, Cynthia Garcia Coll, and Vonnie C. McLoyd, Editors.)

Implications for a children's perspective	The authors explore the extent to which poverty affects developmental outcomes and, in turn, reduces children's opportunities for success and happiness in adulthood.
Study design	The authors linked two data sets to do their analysis. They used longitudinal data from the Panel Study of Income Dynamics (PSID) to describe patterns of family and neighborhood poverty and their effects on success in adolescence. They used longitudinal data from the Infant Health and Development Program (IHDP) to examine links between economic deprivation and children's

development. (The IHDP is an eight-site randomized clinical trial designed to test the efficacy of educational and family support services and high-quality pediatric follow-up in reducing developmental delays in low-birthweight infants.) Child cognitive outcomes were measured at age five using the Wechsler Preschool and Primary Scale of Intelligence (WPPSI) and the Revised Child Behavior Profile (RCBP). (Please see acronyms in the glossary for a more complete description of data sets.)

Relevant findings

- **Differences were found between black and white families' exposure to poverty, as well as in levels of neighborhood poverty.** Roughly three-quarters of white children never lived in poor families, while only one-third of Blacks escaped family poverty. More than three-fifths of white but only one-tenth of black children lived in neighborhoods with few poor neighbors. In addition, the incidence of ghetto poverty for Blacks (poverty rates in excess of 40 percent in the neighborhood) was more than 20 times that of Whites.

- **Family-level measures of maternal education, female headship, and low birthweight were related to children's cognitive development and behavior problems.** Birthweight was a significant predictor of IQ, but not of behavior problems. The level of maternal schooling was positively related to development outcomes for children, but single parenthood was significantly related to negative child outcomes.

- **Family economic status and the degree of poverty persistence were powerful predictors of children's cognitive development, depression, and aggression.** Increasing the average family income from the poverty line to twice the poverty line was associated with a significant increase in IQ and a decrease in behavior problems. In addition, children in persistently poor families, when compared with never-poor children, have lower IQs and more behavior problems. Differences in family economic status also accounted for most of the detrimental effects of single parenting on IQ, but not on behavior problems.

- **Neighborhood economic conditions also explained differences in behavior problems and IQ between poor and nonpoor children.** Residing in neighborhoods with more affluent neighbors was associated with higher IQ scores, while residing in neighborhoods with more low-income neighbors was associated with children's aggressive behavior.

- **Mothers' positive characteristics and behaviors decreased the effects of poverty on children's development.** The positive learning environment in the home decreased the detrimental effects of low incomes on children's IQ. In addition, healthy psychological functioning of mothers decreased the detrimental effects of low-income children's behavior problems.

Succeeding Generations: On the Effects of Investments in Children. (1994). Robert Haveman and Barbara Wolfe. Russell Sage Foundation, c/o CUP Services, P.O. Box 6525, 75 Cascadilla Street, Ithaca, NY 14851. (800) 666-2211/Fax (800) 688-2877. (331 pp.; $34.95 cloth, $16.95 paper + $3 p/h).

Implications for a children's perspective	The authors evaluate the many background factors—family, social, and economic—that are most influential in determining how much education children will obtain, whether they will become teenage parents, and what their earnings and employment status are likely to be in their twenties.
Study design	The authors used data from the Panel Study of Income Dynamics (PSID). (Please see acronym in the glossary for a more complete description of the data set.) They examined many possible predictors of "attainment," as measured by high school completion, level of education, enrollment in postsecondary education, having a teenage out-of-wedlock birth, receiving welfare benefits, and being economically inactive at age 24, as well as a wide range of family and neighborhood variables.
Relevant findings	• **The more years a parent had of schooling, the greater success their children had in terms of high school completion, higher levels of education, lower likelihood of out-of-wedlock births, lower likelihood of welfare receipt, and increased earnings and employment.** The more years of a parent's schooling increased the probability of teenager's graduating from high school by six percentage points. For children who grew up in a family that had experienced poverty for at least one year, the gain was 10 percentage points; for those who grew up in a deteriorating neighborhood, the gain was 18 percentage points.
	• **Whether the child's family was poor significantly affected the extent of a child's schooling beyond high school, the likelihood of teenage out-of-wedlock childbearing, and the likelihood of future welfare recipiency.** If families of the children had never been poor, the children's level of educational attainment would have increased 3 percent. In addition, probabilities would be reduced that girls would have out-of-wedlock births as teenagers and would be welfare recipients after the birth of these children.
	• **The years a mother worked, and whether a child's family received welfare, also had significant effects on children's school completion, level of education, and later economic activity.** If mothers had worked all ten years when the child was between the ages of six and 15, the high school dropout rate was predicted to drop by 43 percent, average years of schooling to increase by 1 percent, and the probability that children were economically inactive at age 24 to decrease by 45 percent. Further, if participation in welfare by the child's family were to be eliminated, the probability of economic inactivity at age 24 would be reduced by 8 percent, and the average number of years of schooling would be slightly decreased.
	• **Growing up in a single-parent family had large adverse effects on children's "attainments."** If all children could have lived in an intact family throughout their entire childhood, the years of completed schooling would have increased,

and the probabilities of dropping out of school, teenage pregnancies, and welfare recipiency would have all decreased. Further, the number of changes associated with family restructuring (parental separations and remarriages) also affected teenage out-of-wedlock childbearing. There was a 20 percent reduction in the probability of teenage nonmarital births when there was one less parental separation in a family. Conversely, an increased number of remarriages reduced the probability of teenage out-of-wedlock births.

- **Stressful family events and growing up in "bad" neighborhoods also had negative effects on children's "attainments."** Stressful family events, as measured by the number of household moves made by the family, and the amount of time spent living with a disabled head of household, were detrimental to children's schooling, to future labor force participation, and to teenage child bearing. Growing up in a "bad" neighborhood had similar detrimental effects on children's schooling and teenage childbearing.

The Strain of Living Poor: Parenting, Social Support, and Child Mental Health.

(1991). Vonnie C. McLoyd and Leon Wilson. In *Children in Poverty: Child Development and Public Policy*, Aletha C. Huston, Editor, pp. 105–135. Cambridge University Press, 40 West 20th Street, New York, NY 10011. (800) 872-7423 or (914) 937-9600/Fax (914) 937-4712. (331 pp.; $47.95 cloth, $19.95 paper + p/h).

Implications for a children's perspective	The mental health of parents is important because of its implications for child-rearing behavior. This report examines how anxiety and depressive symptoms among single mothers predicts psychological distress among children. It also examines the strategies that mothers adopt to ease economic hardship and the effects of these strategies on their psychological functioning.
Study design	Study participants included 92 children and their mothers, who ranged from age 25 to 58, all of whom were receiving Aid to Families with Dependent Children. These mothers and children separately participated in one-hour interviews in their families' homes.
Relevant findings	• **The study confirmed a significant link between the degree of economic hardship and the mother's psychological distress.** The more efforts the mothers had to make to balance family needs and family income, the more distressed the mothers became.
	• **The mental health status of mothers related to their parenting behaviors.** Mothers under more psychological distress were less nurturant of their children and perceived their parenting roles as more difficult than mothers experiencing less psychological distress.
	• **Economic hardship was not found to be directly related to the level of stress for children. However, it was related to the mothers' psychological functioning, which in turn, was closely related to the level of stress for children.** This implies that "how" mothers coped with economic hardship

(such as cutting back on expenses, or working more) did not directly affect their children's level of stress.

- **The movement from welfare to work should be seen as a family transition, not just an individual transition.** Many adaptations are likely to occur at the family level rather than the individual level, and the transition from welfare to work affects the daily activities of both mothers and their children. This transition is likely to have indirect effects on children through its effects on the mother's psychological well-being. If the physical and psychological demands, multiple role strain, and other transition pressures are not counterbalanced by psychological and material rewards, such as a meaningful increase in the family's standard of living or in the mother's self-esteem, the transition may actually have a negative effect on a mother's psychological functioning.

Growing Up with a Single Parent: What Hurts, What Helps. (1994). Sara McLanahan and Gary Sandefur. Harvard University Press, 79 Garden Street, Cambridge, MA 02138. (800) 448-2242 or (617) 495-2480/Fax (800) 962-4983 or (617) 495-5898. (192 pp.; $19.95 + $3.50 p/h).

Implications for a children's perspective	The authors demonstrate the connection between family structure and children's prospects for success. The authors also examine whether or not children of single parents would have been better-off if they lived with both parents.
Study design	The authors analyzed evidence from four nationally representative data sets; National Longitudinal Survey of Youth (NLSY), Panel Study of Income Dynamics (PSID), High School and Beyond (HSB), and the National Survey of Families and Households (NSFH), including three longitudinal surveys and one survey with retrospective data on children's living arrangements during their upbringing. They examined several outcomes, including high school grades, graduation, college attendance and graduation, early childbearing and marriage, and early labor force attachment. All of the study results were adjusted for differences in race, parents' education, family size, and region of the country. (Please see acronyms in the glossary for a more complete description of data sets.)
Relevant findings	• **Children from one-parent families experienced lower levels of academic achievement than children from two-parent families, as measured by school performance, high school graduation, and college attendance and graduation.** The authors consistently found that children from one-parent families were about twice as likely as children from two-parent families to drop out of high school. For example, data from the NLSY showed that the dropout rate for children from single-parent families was 29 percent, versus 13 percent for children from two-parent families. Prior to dropping out, children from single-parent families did less well on four out of five indicators of school performance. They had lower test scores, lower expectations about college, lower grades, and poorer attendance records; yet they were just as likely as

children from two-parent families to report that they liked school and wanted to go to college. In addition, children from single-parent families show poor educational attainment beyond high school. They were significantly less likely to enroll in college and, if they did enroll, they were less likely to graduate.

- **Both young men and young women from single-parent families were more likely to have reduced labor force attachment after high school than those from two-parent families.** Young men from single-parent families were about 1.5 times more likely to be idle after high school than young men from two-parent families. This pattern held up even after reducing the sample to only those who graduated from high school and after adjusting for test scores, showing that these differences occurred even among subjects of similar abilities. Young women from single-parent families were also found to be at higher risk for reduced labor force attachment.

- **Growing up in a disrupted family increased the risk of becoming a teenage mother by a substantial amount.** This was true whether or not the teenager was married. The increased risk varied from an additional five percentage points in one study to 17 percentage points in another.

- **Little evidence supported the hypotheses that the cause of single parenthood—being divorced or never marrying—or the timing and duration of single parenthood made a difference in children's well-being.** In general, young people from disrupted families were more likely to drop out of high school and were more likely to become teenage parents, irrespective of whether these mothers were never married or divorced, and irrespective of whether mothers married or remarried. There were, however, a few exceptions: children raised by widowed mothers were less likely to drop out of high school or become teenage parents, and boys born to unmarried mothers were more likely.

- **Variations in family income explained a substantial amount of the differences between children of single-parent and two-parent families in the areas of high school dropout rates, teenage parenting, and idleness.** The risk of dropping out of high school for children from single-parent families dropped from 6 percent to 3 percent after accounting for family income. The pattern for teenage childbearing and idleness was similar.

- **Parenting practices also played a large role in explaining the differences between single-parent and two-parent families in child outcomes.** Parenting practices as measured by parental aspirations, involvement, and supervision, accounted for over half the differences between the two types of family structure in high school dropout and teenage childbearing. In addition, parenting practices accounted for all of the difference in idleness between boys in single-parent families and two-parent families. The authors found that these relationships were not because of a loss in income associated with family disruption; they found no relationship between parenting practices and family income.

- **The frequency with which families moved played an important role in explaining differences between single-parent and two-parent family child outcomes.** Mobility was a more important factor than the amount of parental resources.

Profiles of Adults on AFDC

"Poor women have experienced more frequent, more threatening, and more uncontrollable life events than the general population, situations that lead to depression and other mental health conditions."

—See *Poverty and Women's Mental Health* annotation.

Welfare That Works: The Working Lives of AFDC Recipients. (1995). Roberta Spalter-Roth, Beverly Burr, Heidi Hartmann, and Lois Shaw. Institute for Women's Policy Research, 1400 20th Street, NW, Suite 104, Washington, DC 20036. (202) 785-5100/ Fax (202) 833-4362. (86 pp.; $19).

Implications for a children's perspective	The study focuses on work and family income. It analyzes the factors that increase the likelihood that single parents receiving Aid to Families with Dependent Children (AFDC) also engage in paid employment, the kinds of jobs they obtain, and their ability to move out of poverty by combining work and welfare receipt. The study does not identify factors related to children directly.
Study design	This study used the Census Bureau's Survey of Income and Program Participation (SIPP). (Please see acronym in the glossary for a more complete description of the data set.)
Relevant findings	• **The majority of AFDC recipients participated in the labor force over a two-year period or spent substantial time seeking jobs.** Only one-fourth were totally dependent on AFDC and supplementary public assistance programs such as food stamps. Seventy percent of AFDC recipients participated in the labor force during the two-year survey period. Over 40 percent engaged in substantial hours of paid employment, either cycling between AFDC and work or simultaneously combining these two income sources. Another 30 percent spent substantial time looking for work. • **Recipients used AFDC for many reasons, including to supplement low-wage work or to provide a safety net during periods of unemployment, disability, or family crisis.** The average earnings of an AFDC mother provided her with one-third of her family's income; AFDC, food stamps, and the Special Supplemental Food Program for Women, Infants and Children (WIC) provided another 30 percent. For those individuals who were not working, AFDC, food stamps, and WIC provided 60 percent of income. • **Several factors—related to health status, job availability, education, and child care needs—increased the likelihood that a woman on AFDC would work.** These factors included: not being disabled; living in states with low rates of unemployment (3.5 percent or less); less need for expensive child care

(as for infants and toddlers); more education (high school diploma), job training, and prior work experience; and the availability of other financial resources such as child support.

- **Several factors—related to education, work, and the availability of other resources—increased the likelihood that these individuals could move out of poverty.** These included high school graduation; more job training; higher job stability (regardless of the reason why a mother started or stopped working); living in a state that has a low unemployment rate; belonging to a union; receiving income from other household members; and living in a state with relatively high AFDC benefits.

The Health, Earnings Capacity, and Poverty of Single-Mother Families. (1993). Barbara L. Wolfe and Steven Hill. Institute for Research on Poverty, University of Wisconsin, 1180 Observatory Drive, 3412 Social Science Building, Madison, WI 53706. (608) 262-6358/Fax (608) 265-3119. Reprinted from *Poverty and Prosperity in the USA in the Late Twentieth Century.* (1993). B. Papadimitriou and Edward N. Wolff, Editors. New York, NY: Macmillan, pp. 89–120. (16 pp., IRP Reprint Series No. 703; $2).

Implications for a children's perspective	This study analyzes the health status of single women receiving Aid to Families with Dependent Children (AFDC), and the impact of health on their earnings capacity. This information is important for understanding the limitations of welfare-to-work strategies for children with disabled mothers.
Study design	Using the Survey of Income and Program Participation (SIPP), researchers examined the health status of single mothers compared to other women and estimated their earnings capacity—which would be the amount single mothers would earn if they joined the workforce full-time, taking into account their health status and their children's health status. Researchers also used the Current Population Survey (CPS), a larger sample, as a comparison or source of validation. (The first two findings are based on CPS estimates.) (Please see acronyms in the glossary for a more complete description of data sets.)
Relevant findings	• **Seven percent of single mothers had substantial health problems (such as the presence of a disability or the presence of a health problem) that prevented or limited the amount of work that they could do.** The authors' analysis indicated that even if these mothers were to work, they would not be able to earn enough to provide adequately for their children. Many of the women who worked could not find employment with health insurance coverage.
	• **Ten percent of single mothers receiving AFDC reported a disability or health problem that limited work.** Older single mothers (aged 45 to 60) receiving AFDC reported the poorest health, with 41 percent of them reporting health so poor that it limited their ability to work.

- **Single women who reported poor health had significantly lower earnings capacity than women who reported good health.** The annual average earnings capacity of single mothers (in 1984 dollars) was $9,117. The average earnings capacity for a single woman reporting poor or fair health was $2,440. The average earnings capacity of a single mother with a disabled child was $8,135.

- **One hundred percent of families of single mothers in poor or fair health would be poor if they had to rely solely on the earnings capacity of the mother.** In contrast, 22 percent of families with single mothers in good health would be poor if they relied on mother's earnings capacity alone. (These figures did not take child care expenditures into account.)

Poverty and Women's Mental Health. (1990). Deborah Belle. *American Psychologist*, 45 (3), pp. 385–389.

Implications for a children's perspective	The article summarizes former research that shows an association between poverty and mental health status among women. The findings are significant because other studies show that depression and other mental health disorders affect adult parenting behaviors and have an adverse effect on the well-being of children.
Relevant findings	• **Studies have documented high levels of depressive symptoms among women experiencing chronic stressful conditions, particularly economic stress.** One nine-year study found that inadequate income was associated with an elevated risk of depressive symptoms.
	• **Single-parent status, lack of employment, and lack of a college education were associated with mild, chronic depression.** One study showed that nearly half of the low-income mothers had significantly more depressive symptoms than the norm for their communities. Within that sample, unemployment, low-income, and single-parent status were associated with the extent of depressive symptoms.
	• **Poor women have experienced more frequent, more threatening, and more uncontrollable life events than the general population, situations that lead to depression and other mental health conditions.** Crime and violence, child illness and death, and imprisonment of husbands and partners are some examples. Poor women also face persistent, undesirable chronic conditions such as inadequate housing, dangerous neighborhoods, burdensome responsibilities, and financial uncertainties.

ECONOMIC ISSUES FOR FAMILIES LEAVING WELFARE FOR WORK

"It has long been recognized that "contacts" are crucial in getting higher skilled and better paying jobs. This new research suggests that contacts are important even in the low-wage sector of the economy. AFDC recipients, who tend to be more isolated from job networks than people who have been working, are more likely than others to be rejected when they search for work."

—See Finding Work in the Inner City annotation.

Finding Work in the Inner City: How Hard is it Now? How Hard Will it be for AFDC Recipients? (1995). Katherine Newman and Chauncy Lennon. Russell Sage Foundation, 112 East 64th Street, New York, NY 10021. (212) 750-6038/Fax (212) 371-4761. (17 pp., Russell Sage Foundation Working Paper No. 76; Free).

Implications for a children's perspective	This study focuses on minority workers' employment opportunities in the low-wage fast-food industry in Harlem. The research compares the skills and education levels of these workers and recipients of Aid to Families with Dependent Children (AFDC). An understanding of the low-wage market is important for predicting economic prospects for families leaving AFDC for work.
Study design	The authors tracked the employment histories of 200 people who work in the fast-food industry in Harlem—mostly African Americans, immigrants from the Dominican Republic, Puerto Rico, and other parts of the Caribbean. They also studied 100 people who applied for these minimum wage jobs but were turned down. Intensive interviews helped the investigators make comparisons between those individuals chosen by employers and those rejected.
Relevant findings	• **Younger applicants, especially those under the age of 20, had a harder time than others getting entry-level jobs.** New hires were disproportionately older than 20, with the largest number of workers aged 25 and over. Older workers had moved into a labor market that was, not long ago, reserved for youth. • **African Americans were at a disadvantage in the hiring process compared to other groups.** Employers showed a preference for applicants who were not African American, even in central Harlem, which has a predominantly African American population. African Americans were rejected at a much higher rate (86 percent) than other groups (62 percent). • **Employers preferred job applicants who were commuting from more distant neighborhoods; they avoided applicants from the immediate area.** The rejection rate (92 percent) was much higher for local applicants than the rate (73 percent) for individuals living farther away, even controlling for race, gender, education, and age.

- **Networks of friends and family members affected a person's success in finding a low-wage job.** It has long been recognized that "contacts" are crucial in getting higher skilled and better paying jobs. This new research suggests that contacts are important even in the low-wage sector of the economy. (AFDC recipients, who tend to be more isolated from job networks than people who have been working, are more likely than others to be rejected when they search for work.)

- **Native-born applicants were at a disadvantage compared to legal immigrants in securing entry-level work.** Despite the fact that Harlem is mostly populated by African Americans, recent immigrants had a better chance of being hired (42 percent) than native workers (14 percent) for fast-food jobs in Harlem, even controlling for differences in education and other variables.

- **Individuals successful in finding work had a considerable amount of work experience before they were hired for the job.** Over 50 percent of new hires older than 18 had found their first jobs when they were younger than 15 years old. (AFDC recipients, many with no prior or recent work experience, would be at a disadvantage when competing for these jobs.)

- **Individuals who had an AFDC recipient in their household (whether themselves or another person) were more likely to be rejected when applying for a fast-food job.** Nearly 89 percent of those with an AFDC recipient in their household were not hired, while only 80 percent of those with no AFDC income were rejected.

- **People seeking minimum wage jobs had made a substantial effort to find a job.** Many people believe that individuals who cannot find jobs are not really trying. Yet this research found that even the youngest people in the market (16–18-year-olds) had applied previously for four or five jobs before applying for the fast-food jobs. The oldest applicants had applied for an average of seven or eight jobs before applying for these jobs.

- **Job seekers had realistic expectations about the wages they were hoping for and would accept.** The average wage sought by those who were rejected from these fast-food jobs was $4.59 per hour. They indicated that they would be willing to accept even lower wages ($4.17 per hour, which is below the legal minimum wage). This was the case even though these job seekers had actually performed much better in the past. The average wage for the best job they had held in the past, $6.79 per hour, suggested that many were suffering from eroding wages.

- **Most AFDC recipients had lower job qualifications than those currently in the labor market.** AFDC recipients had lower levels of education than those currently in the labor market. Thirty-three percent of AFDC recipients, compared to 39 percent of those rejected for the fast-food jobs, and 54 percent of those hired, graduated from high school. Research also suggests that AFDC recipients have less work experience than those currently in the labor force.

- **AFDC recipients were more likely to have young children to take care of than those who had been hired in the fast-food jobs.** Sixty-one percent of the short-term AFDC recipients had a child under the age of three, while only 23 percent of those working had young children. This research suggests that child care problems among working mothers earning low wages contribute to job instability.

When Welfare Ends: Subsistence Strategies of Former GA Recipients, Final Report of the General Assistance Project. (1995). Sandra Danziger and Sherrie Kossoudji, University of Michigan School of Social Work, 1065 Frieze Building, Ann Arbor, MI 48109-1285. (313) 764-5254/Fax (313) 936-1961. (43 pp.; Free).

Implications for a children's perspective	This report analyzes the impacts of the termination of General Assistance (GA) on those it was designed to serve—nonelderly impoverished adults without dependent children. Although the program did not serve children, the effects of GA termination on recipients may suggest what might happen to parents and children who may cease to receive Aid to Families with Dependent Children (AFDC) cash assistance under new program rules.
Study design	This report is based on 426 respondents interviewed two years after the termination of GA in 1991. Issues covered concerned health, program assistance, employment, housing, family, and emotional well-being. Most recipients had significant barriers to employment, including an unemployment rate of 9.2 percent, and 60 percent of the respondents reported chronic health conditions.
Relevant findings	• **Although 76 percent of respondents had previous work experience, only 38 percent had found formal employment in either of the two post-GA survey years.** One-third of jobs held by GA recipients were in manufacturing and came with benefits. Only 12 percent had not worked previously, but did work after the termination of the GA program. After GA ended, janitorial and kitchen work dominated formal job opportunities.
	• **In contrast to the stereotype of an "able-bodied" caseload, former GA recipients reported significant health problems, including high levels of chronic illness and disability and low levels of health care and benefits.** Half of the respondents reported that their health had deteriorated, and 26 percent were enrolled in a disability program. Only 44 percent of the employed had health insurance, while 75 percent of unemployed respondents had medical coverage.
	• **GA itself did not hamper incentives to work.** GA clearly provided a safety net for times when people were not able to support themselves. Forty-three percent of those on GA in 1991 were not enrolled in any state programs two years before, and 44 percent were not enrolled in any programs two years after GA ended.

- **Two-thirds of former GA recipients relied on two or more sources of cash in the month before the survey.** Over a quarter of the sample relied primarily on disability benefits; about 20 percent had their own earnings; 5 percent were receiving AFDC; 4 percent had Unemployment Insurance (UI), Workmen's Compensation (WC), or private pensions; 17 percent depended on casual labor or odd jobs; 7 percent relied on a spouse's earnings or benefits; about 9 percent relied on friends or other family members; and about 12 percent had no cash support from any of these sources.

- **While reliance on family and friends increased over the post-GA period, most respondents suffered.** Over half of the second-year sample were found to be at risk of clinical depression. This finding held for the increased number of GA recipients who lived in doubled-up housing.

- **Some respondents had to resort to more desperate means to get by.** In the second year after termination, 13 percent searched trash cans for food or goods, 18 percent asked for spare change, 18 percent pawned their possessions, 3 percent stole food, and 13–15 percent sold food stamps. About a third of respondents went to local charities for help. Research on homeless shelter services in Detroit suggests that demand greatly overwhelmed available beds.

- **Economic outcomes varied significantly by age and health status.** While more than half of the younger healthy group and the younger chronically ill group had worked in a formal job in the second post-GA year, fewer than one in three older healthy respondents and only one in eight older chronically ill respondents had been formally employed during this period. One-third (40 percent of nondisability respondents) were actively seeking a job, and more than 80 percent of the younger healthy respondents, 75 percent of the older healthy respondents, and 40 percent of the older chronically ill respondents, were in the labor force.

- **Former GA recipients were living on the edge of subsistence, even adding up all cash sources.** In the month preceding the survey, the average respondent had cash sources of $454. The younger chronically ill had higher cash resources than any other group, because of a high level of family support. The older chronically ill fared the worst, with an average of $300 in cash sources in the month before the survey. Thirteen percent of respondents had no cash resources, and 28 percent had between $1 and $299.

- **Most former GA recipients were not doing as well as they had before losing their GA benefits, despite government officials' optimistic predictions.** Ninety percent of recipients who received disability benefits (26 percent of the total group) fared as well after their GA benefits ended; only 35 percent of the younger chronically ill, 32 percent of the older chronically ill, 46 percent of the younger healthy, and 17 percent of the older healthy were faring as well in the month preceding the survey. Removing all government sources of cash, medical assistance, and food stamps, none of the disabled, 7 percent of the younger chronically ill, 2 percent of the older chronically ill, 11 percent of the younger healthy, and 7 percent of the older healthy were doing as well as they had on GA.

PROGRAM STRATEGIES AND THEIR IMPLICATIONS FOR CHILDREN

"Programs successful in providing or coordinating services for children shared common elements, although they implemented their work in different ways. These elements included a coherent mission, established collaborative relationships with other agencies, outreach activities, well-trained and supported staff, and a reliance on funding sources and mechanisms that produced responsive service delivery and accountability."

—See *Poor Children and Welfare Reform* annotation.

Programs to Enhance the Self-Sufficiency of Welfare Families: Pathways of Effects on Young Children. (1994). Martha Zaslow, Kristin Moore, Mary Jo Coiro, and Donna Ruane Morrison. Paper presented at the Welfare and Child Development Workshop, December 5–6, at the National Academy of Sciences, Board on Children and Families. Child Trends, Inc., 4301 Connecticut Avenue, NW, Suite 100, Washington, DC 20008. (202) 362-5580/Fax (202) 362-5533. (30 pp.; $3.10).

Implications for a children's perspective	This paper explores how the range of program strategies to enhance the self-sufficiency of adults receiving Aid to Families with Dependent Children (AFDC) also affect children. The authors consider both economic variables (level of maternal education and family economic status) and noneconomic variables (quality of child care, quality of the home environment, and mothers' psychological functioning).
Study design	The authors reviewed the evidence from the evaluations of seven welfare-to-work demonstrations: Job Opportunities and Basic Skills training program, Greater Avenues for Independence program (GAIN), Even Start Family Literacy Program, New Chance, Comprehensive Child Development Program, Teenage Parent Demonstration, and Project Redirection. These programs all served families on AFDC or predominantly low-income families, and each provided some self-sufficiency services to the parents. Each evaluation involved comparison of an experimental group with either a randomly assigned control group or a matched comparison group. The programs were single-generational, focusing primarily on the economic self-sufficiency of the parent, or two-generational, with program components aiming to enhance the development of the children as well as parental development and self-sufficiency.
Relevant findings	• **Programs of both the single- and two-generation type had effects on earnings and AFDC receipt.** Participants in GAIN, Teenage Parent Demonstration, and Project Redirection had higher earnings and lower levels of AFDC receipt. In addition, GAIN showed some success in moving families out of poverty.

- **The majority of programs reported positive impacts on participation in educational activities and on parental educational attainment.** Five of the six programs that measured parental educational activity found that it increased. In addition, four of the six that included educational attainment found an increase. However, of the three evaluations that measured both educational achievement and attainment, none reported an impact on achievement.

- **Participation in programs significantly increased participation in mental health services or counseling; but beyond participation, the results reflected no measurable gains in mothers' well-being.** Among the three two-generation programs examining participation in mental health services, all reported increases. None of the evaluations reported effects on depression, locus of control, or stress level. However, two programs reported improvements in social support and positive social relationships.

- **Both single- and two-generational programs affected children's participation in child care.** All the programs that measured child care use reported increases. In addition, all of these programs reported increases in the use of formal care arrangements. Two programs also reported an increase in the use of informal arrangements (unregulated care by family, friends, or neighbors).

- **Programs that included a parenting component resulted in significant levels of participation in parenting-related activities, but the measurable results of this increased participation were moderate.** Project Redirection showed improvements on both socioemotional and cognitive measures, including language stimulation in the home, maternal warmth, and maternal acceptance. Three studies (New Chance, the Comprehensive Child Development Program, and Teenage Parent Demonstration) reported that mothers participating in parenting activities were warmer and less harsh in their beliefs or their behavior with their children. Focusing on cognitive measures, participation in Even Start was associated with an increase in the amount of reading materials in the home, but it had no measurable effect on several other cognitive measures.

Poor Children and Welfare Reform. (1992). Olivia Golden. Auburn House, Greenwood Publishing Group, P.O. Box 5007, 88 Post Road West, Westport, CT 06881. (800) 225-5800 or (203) 226-3571/Fax (203) 222-1502. (207 pp.; $42.95 + $4 p/h).

Implications for a children's perspective	The author draws case examples from seven welfare service delivery agencies that make a special effort to include resources for children. She describes how welfare services are currently delivered and how case management and collaboration approaches can improve services to children of adult welfare recipients.
Study design	Seven sites were selected to show success in delivering high quality services to families and children receiving Aid to Families with Dependent Children (AFDC), or to demonstrate close relationships between service delivery and the welfare agency. Program categories included: (1) *teenage parent programs:* Teenage Services

Act Next Step Program, Elmira, New York; GAIN Teen Parent Project, San Diego, California; and Teenage Pregnancy and Parenting/GAIN Collaboration, San Francisco, California; (2) *services to school-age children:* Earhart-Fort Wayne—Jackson—Conner-Warren Dropout Prevention Program, Detroit, Michigan; (3) *services to young children:* Employment and Training CHOICES Voucher Child Care Program and Adult Case Management, Massachusetts and Parent and Child Education, Kentucky; and (4) *services to multineed families:* Integrated Family Services System, Oklahoma.

Relevant findings

- **Significant barriers to serving children and adults existed in traditional human service systems.** These included having a focus on services for individuals rather than family-related services, poor entry points and inadequate outreach, discontinuity, gaps and barriers in service delivery, fragmentation and isolation of services and providers, and a categorical organization of services.

- **The welfare agency was a logical place to provide or coordinate direct services for children from low-income families.** About half of all low-income families were found to receive AFDC benefits in these sites, and welfare agencies came into contact with more poor families than any other organization. In addition, welfare agencies historically both determined eligibility and provided services directly.

- **Programs successful in providing or coordinating services for children shared common elements, although they implemented their work in different ways.** These elements included a coherent mission, established collaborative relationships with other agencies, outreach activities, well-trained and supported staff, and a reliance on funding sources and mechanisms that produced responsive service delivery and accountability.

- **Case managers played an important role in those programs that successfully served children.** Case managers overcame or minimized the effects of a categorical, impersonal system that sometimes created a bureaucratic maze for an often overwhelmed family. Case managers created personal relationships with their clients, allowing them to adjust family needs assessments as they saw children develop and change, to help children by helping their parents, to coordinate direct services to children, and to encourage other service providers to be responsive.

- **The author identified five key challenges for policymakers and program administrators to more effectively meet children's needs.** These challenges included: (1) adopting a broader and longer-term mission that seeks to change the lives of families, even across generations; (2) engaging in collaborations that link the organizations that serve children and families and that work to overcome organizational differences; (3) improving outreach and intake processes to reach appropriate families; (4) providing personalized responsive services; and (5) balancing discretion and accountability.

Two Generation Programs for Families in Poverty: A New Intervention Strategy.

(1995). Sheila Smith, Editor. Ablex Publishing Corporation, 355 Chestnut Street, Norwood, NJ 07648. (201) 767-8455/Fax (201) 767-6717. (288 pp., Advances in Applied Developmental Psychology, Volume 9; $24.50 + p/h).

Implications for a children's perspective	This volume examines several relatively new intervention programs that target low-income families with young children and attempts to integrate two kinds of supports—self-sufficiency services for parents and child development services for children.
Study design	The book describes several two-generation programs, discusses common themes, and identifies areas where additional research is needed. The programs described include the Even Start Family Literacy Program, Avance Parent-Child Program, New Chance, Comprehensive Child Development Program, Head Start Family Service Centers, and the Step Up Demonstration Project.
Relevant findings	• **Two-generation programs targeted a larger range of risk factors than traditional early childhood interventions.** Most traditional early childhood programs provide little support to help parents improve their employment status and income. By providing adult education, job training, and other employment services, two-generation programs may reduce the chance that children will grow up in poverty, a condition associated with multiple risks that can jeopardize children's healthy development. By combining services that provide immediate support for children's healthy development (such as high quality child care) with services that could help families escape poverty (such as education for parents), two-generation programs seek to reduce a large number of risk factors that affect children's development in the early years and beyond.
	• **Current two-generation program models differed from each other on many dimensions of service delivery and structure.** The models examined in the volume all reflected a two-generation strategy, but differed in several ways, including the strength of their child development services, duration of the intervention, and provision of a structured program versus one that is highly individualized. Past research suggests that some of these differences may affect a program's ability to benefit children. For example, failure to provide a direct, sustained early childhood intervention (such as high quality child care or early childhood education) would be expected to reduce the program's capacity to promote children's cognitive development.
	• **Direct comparisons of different two-generation programs and their impacts would be needed to determine the most cost-effective models.** To date, research on two-generation programs has been conducted on individual models. The authors recommended that future research directly compare the effects of different models based on the strongest features of previously studied programs. This approach is needed to determine which program designs are most cost-effective in promoting employment and income gains for parents and good developmental outcomes for children.

Bridging the Worlds of Head Start and Welfare-to-Work: Building a Two-Generation Self-Sufficiency Program from the Ground Up, Revised Edition.
(1993). Toby Herr and Robert Halpern, with Ria Majeske. Project Match, Erikson Institute, 420 North Wabash Avenue, Chicago, IL 60611. (312) 755-2250 ext. 2273 or 2297/Fax (312) 755-2255. (57 pp.; $7.75 + $2.25 p/h).

Implications for a children's perspective	This project links a Head Start program in Chicago with a demonstration project aimed to move welfare recipients toward self-sufficiency. It focuses on the adult-specific goals of increasing self-sufficiency and decreasing dependence on Aid to Families with Dependent Children (AFDC). It differs from many other programs in that it recognizes parental involvement in Head Start as a step toward self-sufficiency.
Program design	The Chicago Department of Human Services, in partnership with Project Match, a community-based welfare-to-work program for residents of the Cabrini-Green housing development in Chicago, created a two-generation Head Start self-sufficiency demonstration project called Step Up. Step Up is an effort to broaden Head Start so that it can function and be viewed as a base for helping the most disadvantaged recipients of AFDC move toward economic self-sufficiency.
Study design	This study tracked the experiences of 47 parents who volunteered to enroll in Step Up during the first six months of the project. These parents wanted to make the transition from Head Start to participation in outside activities such as education and employment.
Relevant findings	• **The initial recruitment strategy to attract participants to the project involved a thoughtful "marketing" of the new self-sufficiency services to the Head Start parents, as well as the phenomenon of self-selection.** After the first six months, 47 parents had enrolled in the demonstration. Twenty-eight (60 percent) of these parents obtained initial placements in school, work, or volunteer positions outside of Head Start. Seven (15 percent) were actively volunteering at Head Start. The other 12 (25 percent) parents were neither participating regularly at Head Start nor actively working with a counselor. • **The project successfully identified a progression of activities and tasks based at the Head Start site to create a generic "within Head Start" ladder toward self-sufficiency for use by other Head Start programs.** Major categories of participation included: supporting the child's development, volunteering, group activities, and family and community advocacy. • **A relationship appeared to exist between a person's capacity to move toward self-sufficiency and her ability to fulfill parenting responsibilities.** Mothers demonstrating support for their child's development appeared to be on the first step toward self-sufficiency. Many of the parents who found it difficult to get to work on time also had difficulty getting their children to school on time. This developmental approach stands in contrast to current welfare-to-work practices in which competencies related to parenting are not viewed as precursors to success on the job or used as job readiness indicators.

- **Volunteering helped participants move toward self-sufficiency, especially if the volunteer experience mimicked the world of work.** An important distinction existed between unscheduled and scheduled volunteering at the Head Start site. A parent who committed to a regular schedule for volunteering was seen as more ready for work even if the "unscheduled" parent volunteered for more hours. Volunteer internships with stipends were created to offer work-like experiences.

- **Group activities such as committees and workshops were a third set of activities that helped participants move toward self-sufficiency.** Parents advanced up the "group activities" ladder by increasing the number of meetings they attended or by taking on more responsibility within groups. Those elected as officers of committees (chairperson or secretary) achieved the highest step on this ladder. A final set of activities involved family and community advocacy, including membership or involvement in school councils, tenant boards, neighborhood watch groups, or Head Start advocacy activities such as planning events and helping with recruitment.

- **Everyone on AFDC could and should be considered actively involved in the interrelated processes of leaving welfare and improving his/her family's lives.** These processes should occur within a flexible time frame because of both personal and labor market factors. Activities not normally viewed as legitimate welfare-to-work placements can be added to the policy framework and used as indicators of effort to move toward self-sufficiency.

- **Keeping parents moving toward self-sufficiency (after their initial placement) required efforts concerning retention, replacement, and help with transition.** Step Up provided post-placement follow-up services to keep parents on the ladder toward self-sufficiency. The Step Up counselor provided the support that participants needed to keep their jobs or complete school, to work with parents not meeting their goals to create more realistic plans, and to help parents ready to move to a higher step on the ladder.

- **A key strategy for making the steps on the ladder toward self-sufficiency legitimate was the creation of a public recognition system for the achievement of incremental gains toward goals.** The rationale for the need for public recognition was that most welfare recipients live in communities where they get little positive feedback. They need messages from their environment letting them know they are "on track" and should keep trying.

Changing What Counts: Rethinking the Journey Out of Welfare. (1991). Toby Herr and Robert Halpern, with Aimee Conrad. Center for Urban Affairs and Policy Research, Northwestern University, 2040 Sheridan Road, Evanston, IL 60208-4100. (708) 491-8712/ Fax (708) 491-9916. (50 pp. + appendices; $4 prepaid).

Implications for a children's perspective	This publication describes research findings from Project Match, a community-based welfare-to-work program located in an inner-city neighborhood in Chicago that serves residents of the Cabrini-Green housing development. The authors offer insights about the long and difficult process of very disadvantaged parents making the transition from Aid to Families with Dependent Children (AFDC) to work. The authors do not consider children's needs directly, but they emphasize the self-sufficiency gains of adults who become more actively involved in meeting their children's needs.
Program design	Project Match, begun in 1985 as a demonstration program of the Illinois Department of Public Aid, has provided assistance to over 600 inner-city residents who volunteered to participate. Key elements of the model include a long-term commitment to participants, comprehensive case management, and a focused mandate on the specific goal of economic self-sufficiency. Assessment and goal-setting are ongoing, and participants receive recognition and positive feedback for incremental gains.
Study design	The authors analyzed the case histories of 225 Project Match participants who had been in the program for three to five years.
Relevant findings	• **Participants worked toward self-sufficiency through ten different routes.** The researchers described six of these routes as "steady progress toward employment," representing 48 percent of participants. They described three routes as "unsteady progress through employment," characterizing 34 percent. The remaining 19 percent were assigned to the general category of "lack of measurable progress."
	• **Some welfare recipients needed to undertake small steps toward self-sufficiency that were not directly tied to employment; they involved community work and parenting commitments.** As a consequence, Project Match developed a career ladder that identified small first steps on the premise that a person is more likely to adhere to a career track if the initial job placement represents a modest extension of what he or she is already doing. Such community activities included volunteering at a child's Head Start center, participating in a parent support group, taking a child to the library, or taking a vocational course. These activities provided a starting point that reflected reasonable initial expectations for the highest-risk families.
	• **The average wage for the group that made steady progress through employment steps was $8.42 an hour.** Nineteen percent of participants, however, plateaued at a much lower average wage of $4.96 per hour.
	• **High-school equivalency classes were not helpful and were an unrealistic first placement for Project Match participants.** After experiencing low-paying,

entry-level jobs with few prospects for advancement, many participants understood the link between school and work. It was only at this point that some were able to make and follow through on a commitment to strengthening basic skills.

Five Years After: The Long-Term Effects of Welfare-to-Work Programs. (1995).
Daniel Friedlander and Gary Burtless. Russell Sage Foundation, c/o CUP Services, P.O. Box 6525, 750 Cascadilla Street, Ithaca, NY 14851. (800) 666-2211/Fax (800) 688-2877. (230 pp.; $34.95 + $3 p/h).

Implications for a children's perspective	This book summarizes the five-year impacts on family income and Aid to Families with Dependent Children (AFDC) expenditures of four welfare-to-work programs evaluated by the Manpower Demonstration Research Corporation (MDRC). Long-term impact estimates are critical to understanding the full effect of a program, indicating whether permanent changes occurred in the lives of enrollees. These evaluations did not measure direct outcomes for children; they focused on family income.
Program design	Three of the four programs evaluated were state-initiated Work Incentives programs evaluated by MDRC between 1982 and 1987 in Virginia, Arkansas, and Baltimore, Maryland. The fourth MDRC-evaluated program was a specially funded federal demonstration in San Diego, California using the Saturation Work Incentive Model. The most common program activity was some form of structured job assistance that provided guidance and structure in job search activities. Participants who failed to find a job could be assigned to three-month unpaid work positions. Education and training were a significant part of the Baltimore and San Diego programs, although neither emphasized immediate assignments to basic education classes.
Study design	The study looked at data from these four social experiments to assess the effectiveness of alternative welfare-to-work strategies over a five-year period. Previous analyses of the four programs had tracked program participants and control-group members for only two to three years.
Relevant findings	• **The five-year earnings of program participants exceeded those in the control group by at least double the net costs of program operations—and they greatly exceeded original two-year findings on earnings.** The five-year impacts were two to four times greater than those observable over the planned two-year evaluation periods, reflecting the importance of a longer-term perspective in assessing total program impact. In Arkansas, participants earned an average of $1,079 more annually than the control-group members. In San Diego, the difference in earnings between the two groups was $2,076. Because AFDC benefit levels were reduced for individuals with earnings gains, the overall financial position of enrollees improved in only two of the four programs.

- **As a result of welfare-to-work programs, participants depended more on their own earnings and less on AFDC for income over the five-year follow-up.** The study did not measure nonfinancial impacts, positive or negative, on these individuals or their families.

- **Individuals who did not participate in welfare-to-work programs (the control group) also experienced considerable gains in earnings.** Control-group earnings approximately tripled from year one to year five in all four programs. Over the same period, AFDC payments for these individuals dropped by one-third to two-thirds. In the fifth year, the differences between control-group members and participants lessened considerably.

- **The main initial impact in all four sites concerned shorter initial spells of joblessness.** The earnings levels and durations of jobs were similar between participants and control-group members; the difference was that participants found jobs sooner. Job-loss rates between experimental and control-group participants were similar.

- **The most persistent long-term earnings impact was associated not with more job finding but with improved on-the-job earnings, possibly the result of skills-enhancement program components.** The most persistent earnings impact, which occurred for Baltimore program participants, was associated with a long-term increase in job earnings. This suggests that a staff assessment approach, going beyond job search and unpaid work assignments to include some education and training, may pay off in longer-term earnings power.

Welfare Realities: From Rhetoric to Reform. (1994). Mary Jo Bane and David T. Ellwood. Harvard University Press, 79 Garden Street, Cambridge, MA 02138. (800) 448-2242 or (617) 495-2480/Fax (800) 962-4983 or (617) 495-8924. (220 pp.; $32 + p/h).

Implications for a children's perspective	This book highlights the past and current research and analyses of the authors and other prominent welfare policy researchers. It focuses mostly on adult-specific goals of increasing income and decreasing dependency on Aid to Families with Dependent Children (AFDC).
Study design	This volume summarizes and interprets information about the dynamics of AFDC use, models for understanding welfare dependency, and lessons learned from several welfare-to-work approaches. It does not describe new research findings.
Relevant findings	• **Welfare receipt was a dynamic process involving mothers with different needs.** Most people who began to receive welfare did so for a brief spell, but the average length of time of those receiving welfare at any point in time was longer, because people with long spells built up the caseload. Many people received AFDC for repeated spells, and for them welfare was a long-term proposition.

- **Many families left welfare for work, although they moved quickly back on welfare.** Different studies of welfare dynamics estimate that 45–69 percent of AFDC "exits" are related to work. Education and previous work experience were powerful predictors of leaving AFDC and obtaining moderate earnings increases.

- **Never-married women were considerably less likely to leave AFDC through marriage than were divorced or separated women; they were slightly less likely to leave AFDC for work.** These differences account for an important part of never-married women's longer durations on welfare.

- **The authors suggest several prescriptions for welfare reform that focus on the continued importance of transitional education, employment, and training services.** The Family Support Act of 1988 embodies these concepts. Two key elements of a successful program are the creation of a vision where there is support and expectation to work or to prepare for work; and the development of a sophisticated approach to defining and monitoring success that recognizes that for some disadvantaged parents, full-time work or education is too high an early expectation, and that smaller milestones should be identified to track individual progress.

- **The authors propose that government policies designed to encourage work and family responsibility will reduce the need for AFDC.** Work should be made to pay, through use of the Earned Income Tax Credit, for example, so that those individuals who work are not poor. In addition, one parent should not be expected to do the work of two, which has ramifications for increased child support and insurance programs. If wider-reaching government policies and programs were to adapt these principles, it would be possible to reform welfare into a transitional, time-limited benefit for those in need.

Welfare Spending in State Budgets. (1993). Sarah Ritchie. Center for the Study of the States, Nelson A. Rockefeller Institute of Government, State University of New York, 411 State Street, Albany, NY 12203-1103. (518) 443-5285/Fax (518) 443-5274. (38 pp.; Request pricing schedule).

Implications for a children's perspective	This paper analyzes state spending on welfare to determine how welfare spending has changed over the last 20 years and to determine how and why state welfare expenditures vary. The information helps to clarify the capacity of states to address the income-related needs of children in families receiving Aid to Families with Dependent Children (AFDC).
Study design	The author reviewed states' cash assistance expenditures over time. She then analyzed state-by-state spending to develop explanations for state variations in welfare spending. The three major cash assistance programs reviewed were AFDC, Supplemental Security Income (SSI), and General Assistance (GA).

Relevant findings

- **Welfare was a small and declining proportion of state budgets.** Between 1972 and 1991, state cash assistance spending increased 160 percent in nominal dollars. In real dollars, however, taking inflation into account, spending fell 18 percent. Meanwhile, real cash-assistance spending decreased over the last two decades as spending for other programs increased substantially. As a result, cash-assistance spending decreased as a percentage of state general expenditures—from 11.2 percent in 1972 to 5.2 percent in 1991. During the same period of time, welfare caseloads increased 128 percent. Some of the developments affecting welfare spending in this time period were under states' control, and some were not. For instance, in 1974 the federal government created the SSI program, which relieved states of a major financial obligation.

- **Medicaid spending grew dramatically over time, which, along with recessions, put fiscal stress on state budgets.** In 1991 alone, Medicaid spending grew 16.9 percent.

- **Welfare spending varied widely across states, with the affluence of a state having a major impact on the generosity of its programs.** States ranged from 9.8 percent of general expenditures for cash assistance (California) to 1.1 percent of general expenditures (North Dakota). The author divided states into five categories in terms of benefit levels, recipiency rates, and poverty rates. Those with high benefit levels, recipiency rates, and poverty rates, included California, Maine, Michigan, and New York. Nineteen states had low benefits, low recipiency rates, and high poverty rates.

- **Recent cutbacks were most severe in states with relatively generous programs.** By and large, these states were hard hit by the recent recession. In 1991 and 1992, 37 states either froze or reduced AFDC benefit levels. States that cut benefits had higher-than-average fiscal stress.

CHILD CARE

"The authors identified a group of home-based caregivers—relatives and nonrelatives—who had a quality they identified as "intentionality," which led to higher quality care. This group of providers were committed to caring for children, sought out opportunities to learn more about child care and education, and sought out the company of other providers to learn from them."

—See *The Study of Children in Family Child Care and Relative Care* annotation.

Caring for Children at the Poverty Line. (1995). Sandra L. Hofferth. *Children and Youth Services Review*, 17 (1/2), pp. 61–90.

Implications for a children's perspective	Child care services are critical to successful efforts to move families from welfare to work. Many parents who have been on welfare, who typically have low levels of education and skills, remain poor for several years even when they obtain employment. This article describes the child care choices, issues, and constraints facing families with preschool children who have incomes below the poverty line.
Study design	The author analyzed data from the National Child Care Survey 1990 and A Profile of Child Care Settings to describe the child care needs and arrangements of working and nonworking poor families (with incomes below the poverty line), working-class families (with family incomes between the poverty line and $25,000 a year), and middle-class families (those with incomes above $25,000 a year).
Relevant findings	• **The need for child care was found to be greater among working poor and middle-class families than in working-class families.** This finding reflected the fact that the majority of parents at all income levels want to care for children themselves. Working-class families were the most likely to have a nonworking parent in the home. (Working poor families included a high percentage of single-parent families, and middle-class families included a high percentage of families with two earners.) Even though more working poor families needed child care than working-class families, fewer actually paid for child care.
	• **Working poor families faced several significant constraints for using day care programs.** Working poor parents were more likely to work odd hours and have changeable schedules. Working poor parents were also more likely to be employed less than full-time, year-round. Since most formal child care programs operated standard business hours and had only full-time spaces available, these programs were largely unavailable to parents working under other conditions. In addition, while the researchers found little difference in perceived availability of care by income, only a fraction of the programs offered sliding-fee scales or

subsidized care—which many working-class parents would need to afford such care.

- **Low education levels were likely to leave nonworking poor parents with limited job opportunities that paid poorly, leading them to use low-priced or free child care.** Thirty-three percent of nonworking poor mothers and 25 percent of working poor mothers had less than a high school education, compared to 17 percent of working-class and 5 percent of middle-class mothers in the sample. Forty percent of working poor mothers were employed in the service sector, compared to 25 percent of working-class mothers and 13 percent of middle-class mothers.

- **After combining direct assistance and assistance from the income tax system (such as the Dependent Care Tax Credit and the Earned Income Tax Credit), 37 percent of nonworking poor, 30 percent of working poor families, 36 percent of working-class families, and 37 percent of middle-class families received child care assistance.** This is because nonworking poor families have access to more direct assistance, while working and middle-income families have access to income tax credits. Working poor families have less access to both of these.

- **The research indicated that the evidence for significant differences by family income in program quality is still weak, although it suggested that children in working-class and middle-class families receive lower quality care than do children from families with lower or higher incomes.** The author cited several recent studies of child care settings in support of this conclusion.

- **The child care decisions of low-income parents appeared to be similar to those of high-income parents. What differed was access, including convenience and the ability to afford the programs.**

Child Care and AFDC Recipients in Illinois: Patterns, Problems and Needs. (1991).
Gary L. Siegel, and L. Anthony Loman. Institute of Applied Research. Distributed by Illinois Department of Public Aid, Child Care and Development Section, 310 South Michigan Avenue, Chicago, IL 60605. (312) 793-3610/Fax (312) 793-4881. (146 pp.; free; *Digest of findings and conclusion*, 36 pp.; free).

Implications for a children's perspective	This volume reports on a comprehensive study of the child care needs of single-parent families with children under age 14 as they try to enter the workforce and leave Aid to Families with Dependent Children (AFDC).
Study design	The population studied consisted of Illinois families receiving AFDC during November 1990. People who had recently left AFDC (due to earnings) were also included in the study sample. The study design involved a survey of 7,000 AFDC recipients, over 100 in-depth, face-to-face, follow-up interviews, 15 focus group discussions, a mail survey to over 1,000 child care providers, and interviews with about 50 other key informants.

Relevant findings

- **Most families using child care relied heavily on informal care. Only one-quarter of those who wanted care in formal facilities had made child care arrangements with child care centers.** Many families wanted other child care arrangements but used informal care because of work hours, subsidy payment mechanisms, or the choice of care available in their communities.

- **The cost of care was the most frequently cited constraint that led many parents to rely on informal care, often provided by relatives.** Without a subsidy or a tuition scholarship, few could afford the cost of center care. The average cost of care reported in the survey of child care centers was $83 a week. This figure was 78 percent of the average cash income of the families in the study population. The more children in a family, the less likely the family could afford the costs of center or licensed family child care.

- **Two out of three (67 percent) single parents surveyed reported that they had no one they could turn to on a regular basis for informal care.** Seventy-five percent lived in households with no other adult present, and 62 percent lived in households with no other adult present nor any child older than 13 years. In these households, therefore, any child care had to be provided by outside sources, including back-up arrangements when problems arose with regular child care arrangements. In addition, one in four reported that there was no other individual inside or outside their household they could turn to for assistance, even on an occasional basis.

- **For many parents, using informal care meant depending on care that was unreliable and inconsistent.** A majority of parents in follow-up interviews using informal care reported they were forced to change child care arrangements within the previous 90 days. Although the changing work hours of the parent sometimes prompted these changes, frequently they became necessary because of changes in the lives of the care providers (such as starting a new job or school, changing work hours, or moving out of the neighborhood), or because the providers could not be counted on consistently. Because much relative and other informal care was unpaid or paid little, parents had little leverage other than good will to sustain the arrangement. Problems associated with informal care and the inability to afford formal center or licensed home care had a direct impact on the ability of these parents to keep a job or complete their school programs.

- **Child care problems prevented many AFDC recipients from working or going to school.** Of the people surveyed, 42 percent said that problems related to child care prevented them from working full-time; 39 percent said that child care problems prevented them from going to school; and 20 percent said they had returned to AFDC within the last year because of difficulties with child care.

- **All recipients of child care subsidies viewed these subsidies as important sources of assistance. Parents who used the Transitional Child Care Assistance program (the one year of child care subsidies guaranteed to families who leave AFDC for work under the Family Support Act) did not return to AFDC as often as those who did not use it.** A significant majority of respondents reported that they would be unable to work or go to school without assistance programs.

GAIN Family Life and Child Care Study Technical Report. (1992). Marcia K. Meyers, Neil Gilbert, and Jill Duerr-Berrick. Family Welfare Research Group, Child Welfare Research Center, University of California at Berkeley, 1950 Addison Street, Suite 104, Berkeley, CA 94704. (510) 642-1899/Fax (510) 642-1895. (228 pp.; $15).

Implications for a children's perspective	This study examines the noneconomic effects (e.g., effects on parenting and child care experiences) of California's Greater Avenues for Independence program (GAIN) on the lives of families receiving Aid to Families with Dependent Children (AFDC).
Program description	The study tracked individuals involved in California's JOBS program, called GAIN. Participants are guaranteed child care if they need it to work or participate in education and training. Each woman chooses, in conjunction with a GAIN worker, to participate in a wide variety of activities: high school general equivalency diploma classes, vocational education and training programs, community college classes, and job search activities. Over time, these individuals frequently participate in more than one activity, sometimes between periods of employment.
Study design	Researchers tracked 255 single-parent AFDC recipients from three counties in California as they entered GAIN between 1989 and 1991. The study explores how these recipients fared as they joined the mandatory welfare-to-work program, began a transition to school and work, and arranged child care during and after program participation. The data provide a detailed look at program experiences from the perspective of participants at three points in time. Researchers collected data through structured telephone interviews before participation, three months after beginning GAIN activities, and 12 months after enrollment.
Relevant findings	• **Sizable numbers of AFDC recipients work or prepare for work even without specially targeted welfare-to-work programs.** At the start of GAIN, 27 percent of the study sample were involved in employment and education activities. An additional 11 percent had worked some hours for pay in the quarter prior to their enrollment in GAIN.
	• **AFDC recipients participated in a variety of work and education experiences, which appeared to have different effects.** Researchers divided these AFDC recipients into three different groups: (1) the remedial group, which tended to have the youngest mothers and the youngest children, and to have the lowest levels of educational attainment and paid work experience; (2) the job-ready group, which tended to have the oldest mothers with the oldest children, more education and more paid work experience; and (3) the vocational group, which fell between the remedial group and the job-ready group in terms of ages of mothers and children, level of education, and paid work experience. The women in the remedial track, who were the most disadvantaged, had the most ambiguous results of the three groups. The women in the vocational group had the most predictable course through GAIN. These women were the most active during the year by several measures. The women in the job-ready group had the most volatile GAIN and employment arrangements. After one year, more of the "job-ready" women (22 percent) had left GAIN and were working than the other groups.

- **Attrition from GAIN was substantial, for both personal and programmatic reasons.** Delays and dropouts occurred because of scheduling difficulties, waiting lists in school or training programs, lack of county funds for child care, or lack of follow-up by GAIN workers (or by AFDC recipients) after an activity was completed. At the end of one year, 58 percent of the sample were involved in GAIN-sponsored school, training, or job-readiness activities, and the remaining 42 percent were again at home full time. A substantial proportion of this latter group appeared to be at home temporarily—in between GAIN components or temporarily out of work or school—and would continue participating.

- **Work experiences were turbulent during the study year, with participants receiving minimal health insurance and child care support.** While 33 percent of the participants worked at some point during the year, by the end of the year only 56 percent of those who had started working were still employed. Median wages reported were $7.29 an hour. Only 27 percent of the jobs held offered health insurance, and fewer than half the women had received subsidized child care.

- **Program attrition was much more likely for women who reduced the amount of time they spent with children or reported increased levels of stress related to conflicting roles of parenting and working or participating in education and training.** GAIN participants who reduced the amount of time they spent with children were one-fifth as likely as others to continue with the program or to get a job by the end of the year. Attrition was also three-quarters higher for women who reported increased levels of role conflict.

- **GAIN helped dramatically reduce child care barriers while the participants attended job preparation activities.** The majority of women reported that prior to GAIN, the lack of appropriate or affordable child care had been a constraint to working or enrolling in school. GAIN participants' use of organized care in day care homes and centers increased when they received child care subsidies. When participants left GAIN (and frequently did not continue to receive subsidies despite eligibility), they relied more heavily on informal child care arrangements.

- **Children experienced repeated disruptions in child care while their parents were enrolled in GAIN activities.** Nearly half of all of these children were in at least two different primary child care arrangements during the year; nearly one-fifth were in three or more different arrangements. The volatility of children's care arrangements matched that of parents' work and training arrangements. For many parents, each transition between one GAIN component and another, or a break in school, meant taking the child out of care, waiting for the new component to begin, and then making new child care arrangements. Problems with the quality and convenience of child care were the cause of one-third of all changes in child care.

- **The adequacy of child care had a significant and substantial impact on whether parents dropped out or continued to make progress in welfare-to-work activities.** Parents were more likely to leave the GAIN program if they were unhappy with the child care program, if their youngest child was in care a long distance from the GAIN activity, if the child care site did not have a sufficient number of caretakers, or if they distrusted the arrangement or considered it unsafe. Those individuals who missed substantial time in GAIN because of sick children or child care difficulties, or who changed their child care often when schedules changed, were also at risk of withdrawing.

Child Day Care in Welfare Reform: Are We Targeting Too Narrowly? (1995).
Marcia K. Meyers. *Child Welfare,* 74 (6), pp. 1071–1090.

Implications for a children's perspective	This study examines the effectiveness of categorical child care subsidies in providing assistance to targeted groups of welfare recipients. The author seeks to learn whether potential recipients are aware of benefits to which they are entitled, whether benefits are limited to target groups, and whether members of those target groups are receiving the benefits.
Study design	The author studied six child care benefits and programs offered in California: Greater Avenues for Independence program (GAIN), Transitional Child Care Assistance program (TCC), Head Start, After School Care, and Dependent Care Tax Credit (DCTC). The study used a subset of 1,343 cases from the California Work Pays Demonstration Survey, which included 15,000 Aid to Families with Dependent Children (AFDC) cases in four California counties. The final analysis was limited to cases where a single mother had at least one child younger than 14.
Relevant findings	• **Most potential recipients were aware of public preschool programs and subsidies for families in JOBS, especially Head Start.** Only 7 percent of parents eligible were not aware of public preschool programs, and only 33 percent did not know about GAIN child care benefits, the single largest source of child care assistance for AFDC recipients. • **Knowledge of other child care assistance was extremely limited.** Nearly two-thirds of AFDC recipients were unaware of the AFDC Child Care Disregard, which if they went to work would allow them to deduct child care expenses from income before calculating AFDC benefit levels. Seventy percent of recipients with school-aged children were not aware of after-school child care, and 85 percent were unfamiliar with subsidies for working poor parents, such as TCC and the DCTC. • **The system of highly targeted child care subsidies was more effective at excluding ineligible clients than including those who needed help.** Only 10 percent of single mothers reported using fully subsidized child care. About a quarter of the single mothers who were enrolled in school, training, or supported job-search activities, used partially or fully subsidized child care for their youngest child. Only 9 percent of those working received fully subsidized care, and only 7 percent received partially subsidized care. Single mothers with paid work hours

fared the worst in their access to child care. Nearly 20 percent of those enrolled in school or training, 29 percent of those combining school and work, and 37 percent of those working full-time paid the full cost of child care themselves.

Cost, Quality, and Child Outcomes in Child Care Centers. Executive Summary. (1995). Suzanne Helburn, Mary L. Culkin, John Morris, Naci Mocan, Carollee Howes, Leslie Phillipsen, Donna Bryant, Richard Clifford, Debby Cryer, Ellen Peisner-Feinberg, Margaret Burchinal, Sharon Lynn Kagan, and Jean Rustici (Cost, Quality, and Child Outcomes Study Team). University of Colorado at Denver, Department of Economics, Campus Box 173364, Denver, CO 80217-3364. (303) 556-4934/Fax (303) 556-3547. (Executive Summary, 17 pp., $8; Public Report, 100 pp., $15; Technical Report, 400 pp., $40 prepaid).

Implications for a children's perspective

This study examines the relationships between the costs of center-based child care, the quality of children's child care experiences, and the effects of child care on children. Successful welfare-to-work strategies will cause more children to be in nonparental care while their mothers work. This study increases the understanding of the impact of child care quality on children's growth and development.

Study design

The research team collected cost and quality data through visits to 50 nonprofit and 50 for-profit centers in California, Colorado, Connecticut, and North Carolina. Researchers used data on 826 preschool children to explore how their developmental outcomes related to their child care experiences. Quality of child care was rated on a scale of one to seven, with "one" signifying inadequate care, "three" minimal care, "five" good care, and "seven" excellent care.

Relevant findings

- **Child care at most centers in the U.S. was found to be poor to mediocre in quality, with almost half less than minimal quality.** The mean score for centers in the study was a four, a full point below the good quality level. Quality of child care for infants and toddlers was of particular concern.

- **Across all levels of maternal education and child gender and background, children's cognitive and social development were positively related to the quality of the child care experience.** Children in higher quality classrooms showed greater receptive language ability and pre-math skills, and had more advanced social skills. Quality of care had an even greater impact on the receptive language ability of minority children and on the self-perceptions of children of less educated mothers.

- **Quality of child care was primarily related to higher staff-to-child ratios, staff education, and the administrator's prior experience.** Staff-to-child ratio was the most significant determinant of quality. Teachers' wages, education, and specialized training also distinguished differences between poor, mediocre, and good quality centers.

- **States with more demanding licensing standards had fewer poor quality centers than those with lower standards.** More poor quality centers were found in North Carolina than the other three states; North Carolina had the least stringent child care standards of the four. Centers that met standards beyond those required provided higher quality services.

- **Three specific types of centers provided higher-than-average quality services because of extra resources that they used to increase quality.** Centers operated by public agencies, centers with public funding tied to higher standards, and worksite centers provided higher quality care than others. They also had higher expended costs and total revenues per child hour, more donated funds, and lower reliance on parent fees. Payments from government and philanthropies made up about 28 percent of revenues.

- **Center child care, even mediocre quality care, was costly. However, the marginal cost to improve the quality of child care from mediocre to good was relatively low.** Average expended costs were $95 per week per child for mediocre care. Although it would only cost about 10 percent more to provide good quality services, the study found that a 10 percent increase would by no means guarantee quality because parents had difficulty recognizing and demanding quality services. A family's average annual costs for child care represent 8 percent of 1993 median U.S. family income for families with two workers, and 23 percent for families with one worker.

- **Evidence suggested inadequate consumer knowledge created market imperfections and reduced incentives for some centers to provide good quality care.** Parents substantially overestimated the quality of services their children were receiving; 90 percent of parents rated their child care center as very good, while trained observers found that most of these programs were poor to mediocre. Parents, while valuing good quality services, apparently did not have the information to demand it. To the extent that government agencies involved in purchasing child care for low-income children offered low payments, or failed to provide higher reimbursements for higher quality, they contributed to lowering the demand for good quality child care.

Early Childhood Centers: Services to Prepare Children for School Often Limited. (1995). Report to the Ranking Minority Member, Senate Subcommittee on Children and Families, Committee on Labor and Human Resources, U.S. Senate., U.S. General Accounting Office, P.O. Box 6015, Gaithersburg, MD 20884-6015. (202) 512-6000/Fax (301) 258-4066. (104 pp.; Report No. GAO/HEHS-95-21; free).

Implications for a children's perspective	This study examines early childhood services to disadvantaged children ages three and four in the U.S. (defined as children in families whose incomes are at or below 185 percent of the federal poverty line). It identifies the services disadvantaged children need to prepare for school, the extent to which they

receive these services from early childhood centers, and the reasons early childhood centers may not provide all the services these children need.

Study design

The Senate Subcommittee on Children and Families requested a study of center-based federal and state early childhood programs. The authors of this study reviewed current literature, consulted with experts, and reviewed standards for early childhood centers. They also analyzed Mathematica Policy Research data from a national sample of early childhood centers to determine whether differences existed in services provided by different kinds of centers. The study also focused on early childhood programs in four states (California, Louisiana, Maryland, and Michigan) to take a closer look at services for disadvantaged children. The authors conducted interviews with state and local administrators in these states.

Relevant findings

- **Developmentally appropriate, high quality, early childhood services helped prepare children for school.** Data showed that high quality services were characterized by having teachers with more education or specialized training, a low child-to-staff ratio, small group size, low teacher turnover, and a planned curriculum that included daily and long-range plans.

- **Parent services at early childhood centers helped prepare children for school.** Parent involvement in children's learning was an important element in preparing children for school. Children who received encouragement and support from their parents were more likely to develop confidence and an expectation that they could succeed in school. Parent services at centers facilitated parental contact by offering meetings with parents, involving parents at the child centers, supporting parents' development through high school general equivalency diploma or training opportunities, and visiting children's homes to help parents expand on their children's center educational experience. Because more and more parents work, researchers and child care providers have also begun to view full-day programs as a critical parent service.

- **Health care and nutrition services helped prepare children for school.** The literature on early childhood development has documented the importance of health care and nutrition to children's development and school achievement. Children in poor health may be absent from school more often than others or less able to perform in class, or they may exhibit disruptive behavior. Untreated injuries or illnesses can lead to permanent disabilities, and poor nutrition adversely affects children's ability to learn.

- **Disadvantaged children, who would benefit the most from attending early childhood centers, were found to be the least likely to attend them.** Sixty-five percent (1.8 million) of disadvantaged children did not attend early childhood centers in 1989. Head Start served just 29 percent of all eligible 3- and 4-year-old children in 1993. Instead of attending early childhood centers, many disadvantaged children stayed at their own home or in another home.

- **Many disadvantaged children attended centers that provided limited services.** Among disadvantaged children who attended early childhood centers, 59 percent attended centers that were less likely than Head Start centers to provide the full range of child development, parent, and health services. For-profit and nonprofit centers were more likely to lack child development services compared with other kinds of centers. School-sponsored and Head Start centers were more likely to provide services important to child development. Both parent services and health services were less likely to be available in centers other than Head Start.

- **Limited places and subsidies impeded centers' efforts to provide education and services to disadvantaged children.** In every low-income census tract visited, the authors found at least one center with a waiting list. Even when places were available, inadequate child care subsidies made it difficult for parents to enroll their children in early childhood centers. In 1991, California had 255,000 children waiting for subsidized care.

- **Narrow program missions constrained provision of services for disadvantaged children.** The mission of the federal programs that subsidize child care is to provide care so that parents can work or attend school or training for employment. Often, subsidies to parents have been so low that parents may have needed to enroll their children in centers that offered fewer services. Parents may also have had to choose centers that did not provide a full range of services because of their need for full-day child care. Nonprofit and for-profit centers were much more likely to offer full-day care than Head Start and school-sponsored centers. Unfortunately, they were also less likely to provide a full range of child development, parent, and health services. The mission of school-sponsored programs originally focused on child development, but recent evidence suggested that these programs were recognizing the importance of a full range of full-time services.

- **Allocation of scarce resources reinforced centers' narrow missions.** Each center tended to devote resources to those aspects of children's needs related most closely to its mission. Scarcity of resources prevented many centers from providing the range of services they wanted to offer. Several state and school district officials in Maryland and Michigan complained that they lacked the resources needed to offer the many services they are supposed to provide. Even Head Start centers faced resource scarcity despite their mandate to meet all needs of children served.

- **Differences in programs that reflected narrow missions served as barriers to collaboration between centers.** Rigidity of funding streams and regulations, and marked variations in salaries and benefits, inhibited the development and management of programs attempting to broaden their services to meet the multiple needs of children and families.

- **State and local initiatives expanded the range of services provided at centers.** California's State Preschool Program and General Child Care and Development Program required all centers to offer a range of services and to establish links with health and social service agencies. In Maryland, Head Start classrooms were created within child care centers. This enabled Head Start children to receive full-day care and allowed the child care center to benefit from the training and resources shared with Head Start.

The Florida Child Care Quality Improvement Study, Interim Report. (1995). Carollee Howes, Ellen Smith, and Ellen Galinsky. Families and Work Institute, 330 Seventh Avenue, 14th Floor, New York, NY 10001. (212) 465-2044/Fax (212) 465-8637. (44 pp.; $9).

Implications for a children's perspective	This study examines how Florida's new teacher-to-child ratios and staff education requirements affect the quality of early education and care and children's development. Successful welfare-to-work strategies will cause more children to be in nonparental care while their mothers work. This study sheds light on factors which will increase the quality of child care programs.
Study design	Three substudies constituted this research project. The data came exclusively from *The Children Study* component, with a sample of approximately 150 licensed child care programs in four counties in Florida: Pinellas, Duval, Broward, and Hillsborough. Overall, 40 percent of the programs served low-income children, 55 percent were nonprofit, and 85 percent were urban. Within each center, three classrooms were selected (an infant, a toddler, and a preschool), for a total of 450 classrooms. Within the three classrooms, one boy and one girl were selected, for a total of 880 children.
Relevant findings	• **After Florida's regulatory changes were implemented, which increased teacher-to-child ratios and training hours, children's intellectual and emotional development improved.** Children were more proficient with language and had fewer behavior problems than before the regulatory changes. The children were observed engaging in more complex play with objects and with each other. They were also more securely attached to their teachers.
	• **Teacher sensitivity and teacher responsiveness also increased after these changes, and negative management styles declined.** Teachers were less likely to respond to a child's misbehavior by yelling, scolding, threatening, or hitting. The frequency of negative management was reduced by 75 percent in some programs.
	• **The numbers of children in growth-enhancing early childhood arrangements increased significantly after the regulatory changes.** The Harms-Clifford measure of overall quality found that between 1992 and 1994 the percentage of children in child care that enhanced their growth and development increased from 25 percent to 36 percent for infants and toddlers, and from 27 percent to 44 percent for preschoolers. The percentage of children receiving "inadequate" care decreased significantly during the same period.
	• **The more stringent the teacher-to-child ratios were in child care programs, the better the children's development.** Children in classrooms out of compliance with Florida's required ratios engaged in less cognitively complex play than did children in classrooms in compliance with Florida's ratios or with professionally recommended ratios (which are even higher than Florida's). Children in classrooms that met professionally recommended ratios engaged in more elaborate play with other children and had higher adaptive language scores than children either in compliance or out of compliance with Florida's

ratios. Similarly, teachers in classrooms meeting professional ratios were more likely to be sensitive and responsive, and less likely to use negative management behaviors.

- **Despite concerns that the new licensing regulations would prove burdensome to programs, no change occurred in the number of children served, and average program size remained constant.** The number of staff employed at programs increased slightly. At the same time, slight increases in teachers' salaries and parent fees responded to cost-of-living increases. Just less than half of the programs (49 percent) raised their fees between 1992 and 1994. The average increase in parent fees was 7 percent over these two years, approximately equal to the cost-of-living change.

The Study of Children in Family Child Care and Relative Care: Highlights of Findings. (1994). Ellen Galinsky, Carollee Howes, Susan Kontos, and Marybeth Shinn. Families and Work Institute, 330 Seventh Avenue, 14th Floor, New York, NY 10001. (212) 465-2044/Fax (212) 465-8637. (133 pp.; $18 + $3.50 p/h).

Implications for a children's perspective	This study is the first sizable observational study of family child care and relative care since 1981. Care in the home of a provider is the most prevalent form of child care for young children with employed mothers in the United States today. Many families that move from welfare into low-wage jobs are likely to rely on this form of child care.
Study design	The study sample consisted of 820 mothers and 225 of their children who received care in the homes of 226 providers in three communities: San Fernando/Los Angeles, California; Dallas/Fort Worth, Texas; and Charlotte, North Carolina. (Out of the total number of providers for the 820 families, 226 agreed to participate in the study.) Researchers interviewed both mothers in the sample and the 226 providers. For each provider, one child from the family was observed in the provider's home.
Relevant findings	• **Parents and child care providers agreed about the most essential components of child care quality.** These components were the child's safety, the provider's and parent's communication about the child, and a warm attentive relationship between the provider and child.
	• **A warm and attentive relationship between provider and child, as well as global quality of care, were found to be positively related to children's development.** This finding was true regardless of whether the children were cared for by regulated or nonregulated providers or relatives.
	• **Providers found to have one positive characteristic were likely to have others.** These positive characteristics included whether providers were committed to taking care of children and were performing the work out of a sense that the care is important (as opposed to providers caring for children to

"help out" the child's parent); and whether they sought opportunities to learn about children's development.

- **Only 9 percent of the providers in this study were rated as good quality providers (meaning growth-enhancing). Fifty-six percent were rated as providing adequate custodial care (neither growth-enhancing nor growth-harming); and 35 percent were rated as inadequate (growth-harming).** The authors pointed out that these findings did not appear to be unique to family child care and relative care. Other studies have indicated the same concerns about quality in center-based care.

- **Children were not more or less likely to be "securely attached" to providers who were relatives than to nonrelatives.** (Security of attachment is a measure of the quality of the relationship between the caregiver and the child.) The authors offered two explanations for finding that care from a relative is not necessarily better than care from a nonrelative. First, 65 percent of relatives in the sample were living in poverty and, as a consequence, were living stressed, socially isolated lives. Second, 60 percent of the relatives were taking care of children to help out the mothers—not because they wanted to care for children.

- **The authors identified a group of home-based caregivers—relatives and nonrelatives—who had a quality they identified as "intentionality," which led to higher quality care.** This group of providers were committed to caring for children, sought out opportunities to learn more about child care and education, and sought out the company of other providers to learn from them.

- **Child care providers regulated by their states, who reported charging higher rates and following standard business and safety practices, were more likely to be sensitive and responsive.** The authors suggested that being regulated could be seen as another aspect of "intentionality." (Regulated providers, who are likely to have been trained and to be "intentional" in other ways, charge more and are also more likely to follow standard safety practices.)

CHILD HEALTH

"Incremental expansions of the Medicaid program continued to be the primary way states extended coverage to additional groups of pregnant women and children. States used statutory program options, allowing expansion of Medicaid eligibility to pregnant women and infants up to 185 percent of the poverty level, as well as other provisions, to further expand coverage for these groups and for older children."

—See *State Initiatives to Provide Medical Coverage for Uninsured Children* annotation.

Child Health and Poor Children. (1992). Sara Rosenbaum. *American Behavioral Scientist*, 35 (3), pp. 275–289. (Special issue: The Impact of Poverty on Children. Jill E. Korbin, Editor).

Implications for a children's perspective	Children's changing access to health care is closely tied with Aid to Families with Dependent Children (AFDC) receipt. This article provides an overview of issues of low-income children's health status.
Study design	The author summarizes prior research on basic indicators of child health, reviews the U.S. Surgeon General's maternal and child health goals for 1990, and discusses the importance of investments in preventive and basic health care to improve children's health.
Relevant findings	• **Poor progress in improving child health can be seen in nearly every basic child health indicator.** The U.S. has shown a notable lack of progress concerning indicators of child health, such as prenatal care, births to teenage mothers, infant mortality, low birthweight, AIDS among children and adolescents, childhood mortality, and outbreaks of preventable childhood diseases. Between 1950 and 1985 the U.S. fell from sixth place to a tie for last place in its ranking for infant mortality among industrialized nations. In 1988, the U.S. ranked 21st in childhood mortality, with many of these considered preventable deaths. Only an estimated 50–65 percent of 2-year-olds in low-income urban neighborhoods have been properly immunized. • **Of the Surgeon General's 1990 goals for the United States, the nation and most states have failed to meet many of the objectives. Neither the nation nor any state has met the objectives for prenatal care, low birthweight, or immunizations for 2-year-olds.** Trends in the numbers of low-birthweight babies and immunized 2-year-olds have moved in the wrong direction. The author projects that the nation will not meet the 1990 objective for improving prenatal care access until the year 2094. • **Health insurance status is closely linked to family income.** In 1986 one-third of all poor children, including over 40 percent of poor children living in

working poor families were uninsured. Children who lived in an employed family with below-poverty income were four times more likely than other children to lack employer-provided coverage.

- **Modest improvements in publicly funded health insurance programs like Medicaid have not offset the decline in employer coverage.** Although the Medicaid expansions of the 1980s helped about 1 million children, 1.5 million children lost employer-based coverage during the same period. Low Medicaid reimbursement rates led to a tripling of the proportion of private pediatricians (from 26 percent in 1978 to 85 percent in 1989) who placed strict limits on the number of Medicaid-insured children they would see. There was also a 28 percent increase in the number of pediatricians who would not treat Medicaid-covered children.

- **Public programs to improve maternal and child health fared poorly in the 1980s.** Funding levels declined for community health centers and the Maternal and Child Health Services Block Grant (which funds states' efforts to develop services for underserved women and children).

- **Investments in preventive and basic health care for pregnant women and children yield major savings for both families and the nation.** Each dollar spent on providing prenatal care to pregnant women saves more than $3 in the first year of life alone. Similarly, each dollar spent on the Special Supplemental Food Program for Women, Infants and Children for nutrition services to a pregnant woman saves $3 in the first year of a child's life. Each dollar spent to immunize a child saves between $11 and $14.

State Initiatives to Cover Uninsured Children. (1993). Ian T. Hill, Lawrence Bartlett, and Molly B. Brostrom. *The Future of Children,* 3 (2), pp. 142–163. (Special issue: Health Care Reform, Richard E. Behrman, Editor.) The Center for the Future of Children, The David and Lucile Packard Foundation, 300 Second Street, Suite 102, Los Altos, CA 94022. (415) 948-3696/Fax (415) 948-6498. (Free).

Implications for a children's perspective	This article describes innovative programs that seek to extend health insurance coverage to low-income children who are not eligible for Medicaid. It also uncovers new opportunities to use federal Medicaid funds to support these programs. Finally, it highlights the potential role that these programs can play in states' broader strategies to provide universal access to health care for all Americans. This study is significant because families leaving Aid to Families with Dependent Children for work often enter jobs without health insurance benefits.
Study design	This study described the features and early experiences of many new children's health initiatives, beginning with programs that originated in the private sector and continuing with promising public sector initiatives in 11 states.

Relevant findings

- **Blue Cross/Blue Shield Caring Programs for children have been successful in pooling community and private sector resources to provide health care coverage for uninsured poor children who did not qualify for Medicaid.** At the time of the article, Caring Programs had begun in 17 states and were beginning in five more states. Total enrollment in these programs nearly doubled from 1991 to 1992, rising from 21,695 to 39,070 children. While the majority of program funds came from philanthropic donations, some insurance providers matched private donations. Public funds supported Caring Programs in several states, including Pennsylvania, Michigan, Alabama, and Iowa.

- **Despite continued growth, Caring Programs covered only a small percentage of eligible poor children.** The Pennsylvania program, for example, had the largest enrollment of all the plans (6,500 children), but it reached only 11 percent of the estimated eligible children in the program area. Waiting lists for coverage existed in 13 of 17 Caring Programs.

- **In response to the rapidly growing number of uninsured children, some states provided limited coverage that included preventive and primary care services for some children.** Minnesota, for example, used a one-cent increase in the cigarette tax to create the Children's Health Plan. This plan provided limited preventive and primary care services to all children under age 18 in families with incomes below 185 percent of the federal poverty level, including both uninsured and underinsured children. The program originally did not cover inpatient hospital care; it later expanded to cover outpatient mental health services.

- **Several states used the Medicaid program to develop state-funded child health insurance programs that provided comprehensive coverage for uninsured children.** These initiatives built on states' Medicaid programs by providing the same coverage and reimbursement rates as the Medicaid program. They also relied on Medicaid-participating providers to render services. States with these innovations included Vermont, Maine, Washington, and Wisconsin.

- **State experiences suggested that there may be some positive aspects to requiring that families share in the cost of program premiums.** Early state experiences indicated that many families were both willing and able to pay some amount toward the cost of their coverage. Minnesota families reported that the annual $25 per-child enrollment fee created the sense that they were not simply being given a "handout" by the state. However, little information was available about the degree to which fees acted as a barrier to enrollment for some families.

- **The demand for coverage came from many types of families, not only from families with uninsured children. Many children whose parents already possessed insurance, but had inadequate coverage or had extensive cost-sharing requirements, also sought coverage under these new programs.** In Minnesota, roughly one-third of enrollees were children who had been insured already. Further, many children who enrolled came from families in which the parents possessed insurance, suggesting that parents were either not offered or did not purchase employer-based coverage for dependents.

- **A critical flexibility in the Medicaid program provided states with a unique opportunity to capture federal dollars either to support new or to expand existing child health insurance initiatives.** This provision, found in Section 1902(r)(2) of the Social Security Act allows states to dramatically expand the number of low-income children and pregnant women eligible for Medicaid. (The following article discusses the effects of the 1902(r)(2) provision.)

State Initiatives to Provide Medical Coverage for Uninsured Children. (1995).
Christopher DeGraw, Jane Park, and Julie A. Hudman. *The Future of Children*, 5 (1), pp. 223–231. The Center for the Future of Children, The David and Lucile Packard Foundation, 300 Second Street, Suite 102, Los Altos, CA 94022. (415) 948-3696/Fax (415) 948-6498. (Free).

Implications for a children's perspective

This article builds on *The Future of Children* article reviewed in the previous entry. Here the authors examine new state developments affecting health care coverage for children, update the status of programs and describe new initiatives and emerging trends. This study is significant because families leaving Aid to Families with Dependent Children (AFDC) for employment often have to take jobs that lack health insurance benefits.

Study design

This study reviewed and summarized information on state efforts to increase health insurance coverage for low-income children.

Relevant findings

- **Incremental expansions of the Medicaid program continued to be the primary way states extended coverage to additional groups of pregnant women and children.** States used statutory program options, allowing expansion of Medicaid eligibility to pregnant women and infants up to 185 percent of the federal poverty level, as well as other provisions, to further expand coverage for these groups and for older children.

- **A number of states created special programs that focused on pregnant women and children who were ineligible for Medicaid; they often used state funds and encouraged the private sector to expand coverage to these vulnerable populations.** These programs, unlike Medicaid, did not receive federal matching funds, and benefits were often limited to preventive and primary care without covering inpatient care.

- **A larger number of states sought broader waivers of Medicaid rules to allow them to expand federally-funded coverage to adults not normally covered by Medicaid, often in lieu of increasing coverage for additional groups of children.** In the process of extending coverage to low-income adults who were ineligible for Medicaid, benefits were modified and states substituted adult coverage for the coverage of additional children who could have been added without a waiver using 1902(r)(2) options.

- **A recent trend in children's health coverage has involved schools helping families gain access to insurance for their children.** Florida's Healthy Kids

Program offered benefits through a Health Maintenance Organization that covered any uninsured child under age 18 in school. Enrollees paid a sliding scale premium, with state and local governments supplying extra funds. Other states have passed legislation expanding school-based clinics that enhance children's access to health care.

- **The Blue Cross/Blue Shield Caring Programs for Children fill gaps in health insurance coverage for children in low-income families who are ineligible for Medicaid.** Programs providing varying benefit levels have been developed in 23 states across the country.

- **A few states have been in the forefront of health care reform, attempting to extend coverage to most, if not all, of the uninsured.** Medicaid expansions and state-sponsored children's insurance programs have often been fundamental to their reform efforts. Among the leaders are Minnesota and Washington.

FAMILIES WITH TEENAGE PARENTS: STRATEGIES TO INCREASE THEIR LIFE CHANCES

"Intervening after teenagers have become sexually active or have given birth is too late for positive impacts. The Office of Technology Assessment reviewed pregnancy prevention programs and found that no evidence existed of significantly reduced pregnancy rates among teenage girls. . . . At-risk teenage girls could be better served if approaches included early identification and treatment, long-term program commitment, and greater community involvement."

—See *Welfare Dependency* annotation.

New Chance: Interim Findings on a Comprehensive Program for Disadvantaged Young Mothers and Their Children. (1994). Janet C. Quint, Denise F. Polit, Hans Bos, and George Cave. Manpower Demonstration Research Corporation, 3 Park Avenue, New York, NY 10016. (212) 532-3200/Fax (212) 684-0832. (372 pp.; $18 + $3 p/h prepaid).

Implications for a children's perspective	New Chance, a demonstration program in 16 locations in 10 states, tested a program model intended to improve the economic prospects of low-income young mothers and their children's development through a comprehensive and intensive set of services. This report summarizes research findings on the early effects of New Chance participation.
Program design	New Chance participants were a highly disadvantaged group of young women, generally just under 19 years old, having first given birth before age 17. Most were from minority groups; approximately one-third had two or more children; and the majority had a child under age two. Applicants had been out of school for more than two years and had reading skills just above the eighth grade level. New Chance services were offered in two distinct phases. Phase I activities included education services (basic academic skills, and, where appropriate, high school general equivalency diploma (GED) classes), employability development classes (career exploration and pre-employment skills), and personal development services (health education classes, and in some cases, health care services, family planning, and life-skills classes). Phase I also included case management and individual counseling. Phase II activities, designed to begin after participants received GEDs or had been in the program for five months, were more focused on employment. Activities included skills training, work internships, and job placement assistance.
Study design	Investigators undertook a rigorous research plan that included random assignment of a large sample of young women, collection of baseline and extensive follow-up information, exhaustive tracing efforts to locate as many sample members as possible, and rigorous statistical procedures. The study collected information 18 months after the point of assignment to the experimental and control groups.

Relevant findings	• **More New Chance participants received a GED or a high school diploma than did members of a control group.** Forty-three percent of the experimental group, versus 30 percent of the control group, had earned a GED by the time of the 18-month follow-up.
	• **New Chance participants and members of the control group had comparably high rates of births.** More than 25 percent of women in the experimental and control groups had a baby during the follow-up period. Moreover, more than half of each group had conceived, with a higher rate of pregnancy among the New Chance group than the control group.
	• **No program effects were noted for health outcomes, levels of depression, or stress for mothers.** There were no significant differences in the way program participants rated their health status. Nearly half of all of the women in both groups were found to be at risk of clinical depression.
	• **The home environments and health outcomes of children of New Chance participants and of the experimental group were largely similar.** Although overall scores were similar, the children of New Chance participants lived in more emotionally supportive homes, with mothers who demonstrated less authoritarian child-rearing attitudes, than the control-group children.
	• **Employment rates between New Chance participants and the control group converged over time.** On average, members of the control group worked just under two weeks more than New Chance participants. Overall, 43 percent of New Chance participants and 45 percent of control-group members worked in jobs that were brief in duration.
	• **Control-group members earned slightly more than New Chance participants.** On average, control-group members earned a cumulative total of $342 more than New Chance participants during the 18 months of follow-up.

The Challenges of Serving Teenage Mothers: Lessons From Project Redirection.

(1988). Denise Polit, Janet Quint, and James Riccio, Manpower Demonstration Research Corporation, 3 Park Avenue, New York, NY 10016. (212) 532-3200/Fax (212) 684-0832. (32 pp.; $12 + $3 p/h prepaid).

Implications for a children's perspective	This report summarizes the final evaluation for Project Redirection, a program begun in 1980 targeted toward pregnant and parenting teenagers. Areas studied concerned employment, earnings, welfare dependency, and parenting skills.
Program description	Project Redirection was a program for pregnant or parenting teenage girls aged 17 and under who had no high school diploma or general equivalency diploma (GED). The program sought to improve the teenagers' educational, job-related, parenting and life management skills, while at the same time encouraging the girls to delay further childbearing. The program linked teenagers with existing community services and held workshops, peer-group sessions, and individual

counseling. The program also paired each girl with an adult "community woman" volunteer who provided ongoing support and guidance within and outside the formal program structure. The program was initially implemented through community organizations in four sites—the Harlem YMCA in New York; El Centro del Cardinal in Boston; Chicanos Por la Causa in Phoenix; and the Children's Home Society in Riverside, California. During the two years of the demonstration, the sites served 805 teenagers, 56 percent of whom were pregnant with their first child, and 44 percent of whom were already parents. About three quarters of the participants reported that their own mothers had been teenage parents as well. Seventy percent of the teenagers were receiving welfare, either as heads of families or as part of another person's family.

Study design

The Project Redirection impact analysis was based on interviews with several hundred young mothers in the "Redirection" (or "experimental") group, and in the "control" group, who did not participate in the program. (The control group was a comparison group of teenage mothers who fit the Project Redirection eligibility criteria but who resided in different communities.) Four rounds of interviews were conducted: at enrollment and one, two, and five years later. Nearly 700 mothers were interviewed in the first three rounds. At the five-year follow-up, completed in 1987, nearly 300 young mothers were re-interviewed.

Relevant findings

- **At the five-year point, Project Redirection participants had more employment and less welfare dependency than the comparison group, and they appeared to be more competent parents with children who were more developmentally advanced.** The pattern of findings over the five-year period was uneven. At the one-year point, the results suggested that Project Redirection resulted in improvements in education, employment, and fertility. By the two-year point, many favorable results disappeared, some of which became evident again at five years.

- **Project Redirection appeared to encourage young mothers to return to school or stay in school while they were in the program, but there was no ultimate difference in educational attainment between the "Redirection" group and the control group.** For both groups, 48 percent of mothers had received high school diplomas or GED certificates five years after entering Project Redirection (or becoming a member of the comparison group).

- **Although total household income was comparable between the two groups, Project Redirection teenagers accumulated more experience in paid jobs during the first two years of the study, and they may have benefited in other ways.** Project Redirection teenagers tested higher in employability, knowledge, and self-esteem than the comparison group at the two-year point. At the five-year point, 34 percent of the Project Redirection participants, compared to 28 percent of comparison group members, were employed. Project Redirection participants had higher weekly earnings ($68 per week compared to $45 per week for the comparison group).

- **At the five-year point, Project Redirection teenagers were less likely to live in households receiving welfare.** Nevertheless, a high percentage of both groups of teenagers relied on welfare, and a low percentage worked for pay. At this point, 49 percent of former Project Redirection participants, compared to 59 percent of the comparison group, were living in households in which someone was receiving Aid to Families with Dependent Children.

- **There were no statistically significant differences in repeat pregnancies between the Project Redirection and the comparison groups.** Because women in the comparison group had a higher number of abortions than women who attended Project Redirection, former Project Redirection participants had more children (an average of 2.4 children in Project Redirection, as opposed to 2.0 in the comparison group).

- **There were several indications that Project Redirection participants gave their children a more positive home environment than the comparison group.** While it appeared that both groups were doing fairly well as parents at the five-year period, some test scores suggested that mothers in the Project Redirection group were providing their children a more positive home environment. In addition, the children of former Project Redirection participants were more likely to attend Head Start and also had better scores on tests that measure vocabulary and assess problem behavior. Neither group showed evidence of maladjustment. However, analyses also indicated that child development outcomes were not primarily the result of increased participation in Head Start.

The Educational Effects of LEAP and Enhanced Services in Cleveland: Ohio's Learning, Earning, and Parenting Program for Teenage Parents on Welfare.

(1994). David Long, Robert G. Wood, Hilary Kopp, and Rebecca Fisher. Manpower Demonstration Research Corporation, 3 Park Avenue, New York, NY 10016. (212) 532-3200/Fax (212) 684-0832. (102 pp.; $12 + $3 p/h prepaid).

Implications for a children's perspective

This report presents new findings on the effectiveness of Ohio's Learning, Earning, and Parenting (LEAP) program in Cleveland, as well as initial results from the Cleveland Student Parent Demonstration. Teenage parents are the population group most likely to become long-term welfare recipients.

Program design

Targeting all of the state's teenage mothers on welfare who had not completed high school, Ohio's LEAP program promotes school attendance and completion by requiring teens in school to attend classes regularly, while those who have dropped out must return to school or enter a program to prepare for the general equivalency diploma (GED) test. LEAP uses bonuses and sanctions to encourage compliance with program requirements. Teenagers receive a bonus of $62 at enrollment and an additional $62 per month for attendance. Teenagers also receive sanctions of $62 per month for poor attendance and failure to attend yearly assessment meetings. The money is added to or deducted from their monthly welfare checks. The program also offers teenagers case management, child care, and transportation assistance.

The aim of the Cleveland Student Parent Demonstration was to assess the effects of enhanced services beyond LEAP. Additional services, provided to approximately half of the LEAP teens, included: school-based activities, such as intensive case management, in-school child care, and instruction in parenting and life skills; or community-based activities, such as outreach, special GED preparation, and parenting and life-skill preparation classes.

Study design	The researchers estimated LEAP's impact by comparing two randomly selected groups of eligible teenagers. The groups were compared in terms of short-term educational outcomes—school and adult education program enrollment, attendance, progress, and completion—and in terms of longer-term outcomes, including employment and welfare receipt. The researcher's sample included 1,392 program participants and 312 control-group members.
Relevant findings	• **LEAP's combination of bonuses, sanctions, and services significantly increased the percentage of eligible teens who completed a high school diploma or GED.** Within three years of follow-up, 21.1 percent of LEAP teenagers had graduated from high school or received a GED compared with 15.5 percent of teenagers in the control group.
	• **LEAP's effect was much larger for teenagers who were enrolled in school when they entered the program than for those who entered as dropouts.** Of teenagers who were initially in school, 29.2 percent had graduated or received a GED, compared with 20.4 percent of the control group, for a gain of 8.8 percentage points or close to a 50 percent increase.
	• **Among teenagers not initially enrolled in school, the effect of LEAP was not significant.** Only 11.1 percent of the teenagers who had been dropouts had graduated or received a GED, compared with 8.6 percent of the control group.
	• **The effect of the enhanced services on school completion—beyond LEAP's own effect—was relatively small for the eligible population as a whole.** All of the impacts of the enhanced services were small and statistically insignificant. The estimated impacts on high school attendance, high school credits, and GED completion were all close to zero. The enhanced services did appear to have been most effective among students who were enrolled in school when assigned. Among the teenagers in LEAP who were initially enrolled, the enhancements increased high school completion rates from 21.3 percent to 25.5 percent.

The Effects of Welfare Reform on Teenage Parents and Their Children. (1995). J. Lawrence Aber, Jeanne Brooks-Gunn, and Rebecca Maynard. *The Future of Children, 5 (2)*, pp. 53–71. The Center for the Future of Children, The David and Lucile Packard Foundation, 300 Second Street, Suite 102, Los Altos, CA 94022. (415) 948-3696/Fax (415) 948-6498. (Free).

Implications for a children's perspective	The paper describes how participation in an "enhanced" welfare program affects teenage mothers' level of self-sufficiency, future childbearing, and parenting, as well as their children's development. Although the study finds few effects of the enhanced services on teenage mothers and their children, it emphasizes that the program's requirement that mothers spend more time out of the home is not harmful for parenting behavior or for child developmental outcomes.

Program description	The Teenage Parent Welfare Demonstration (TPD) was an experiment initiated in 1986 by the U.S. Administration for Children and Families. Investigators randomly assigned teenage mothers entering the welfare system with the birth of their first child to a "regular" services group or to an "enhanced services" group. A total of 6,000 teenage mothers participated in the experiment for up to two years. The enhanced services group faced mandatory school and work requirements and received support services such as counseling, parenting workshops, child care assistance, and education and training opportunities. The regular services group received Aid to Families with Dependent Children (AFDC) as usual.
Study design	A large-scale evaluation of TPD tested the effects of the enhanced services on teenage mothers' level of self-sufficiency at the conclusion of the program. In addition, an Interactional and Developmental Processes Study (IDP) was embedded within the larger evaluation to determine whether participation in self-sufficiency activities had positive or negative effects on parent's behavior with their children, and on the development of the children themselves. Participants in the IDP included 182 African American teenage mothers and their preschool children from Newark, New Jersey.
Relevant findings	• **For the enhanced services group of teenage mothers, rates of participation in self-sufficiency activities were significantly higher than for mothers in the regular services group.** Mothers in the enhanced services group were more likely to be enrolled in school (41 percent vs. 29 percent), somewhat more likely to be receiving job training (27 percent vs. 23 percent), and more likely to have a job at the end of the two-year program (48 percent vs. 43 percent). • **Program involvement yielded little or no significant change in the economic welfare of the teenage mothers except for the specific individuals who became employed.** There was an average $23-per-month increase in earnings from the increased employment of participants in the enhanced services group. In addition, this group averaged $21 per month less in AFDC benefits, and $2 per month less in food stamps. Because of the combination of increased earnings for the enhanced services group and financial sanctions imposed on mothers who failed to participate, the program group received an overall lower level of public assistance. • **Neither participants in the enhanced services group nor the control group were able to secure significant financial support from their children's fathers.** Even though a component of the enhanced program was to help mothers establish paternity and secure child-support awards, there was little difference between the enhanced and regular services groups in the average amount of monthly child support received from fathers. • **There were no differences between the two groups in the number of repeat pregnancies and births.** The enhanced services program did not include specific services, such as family planning, to directly affect this outcome. • **Assignment of the teenage mothers to either enhanced services or regular services did not influence their parenting behavior nor did it directly**

influence their children's developmental outcomes. The mothers in the enhanced services group weren't more positive with their children than the other mothers, nor were they more negative and harsh. Their children did not behave differently during play sessions, nor did they differ on developmental measures such as school readiness (as measured by the Peabody Picture Vocabulary Test and the Preschool Inventory).

- **Although no significant differences were found between the enhanced and regular services groups, differences were found within the enhanced services group concerning the behavior of both the mothers and the children.** The mothers who were more active in self-sufficiency activities were less controlling, less negative, and more engaged when they played with their children than mothers who participated at a minimum level. The children of the more active mothers, in turn, showed more enthusiasm and persistence in completing puzzle tasks.

Welfare Dependency: Coordinated Community Efforts Can Better Serve Young At-Risk Teen Girls. (1995). Report to the Ranking Minority Member, Committee on Finance, U.S. Senate. U.S. General Accounting Office, P.O. Box 6015, Gaithersburg, MD 20884-6015. (202) 512-6000/Fax (301) 258-4066. (104 pp.; Report No. GAO/HEHS/RCED-95-108; Free).

Implications for a children's perspective	This report describes the health and well-being of young at-risk teenage girls and their families, and the condition of the urban neighborhoods where they live. The study describes the local service providers' perspectives on the needs of these girls, how they are addressing those needs, and what obstacles they face in working with the girls, their families, and their communities.
Study design	The authors reviewed the relevant literature, contacted experts on services for at-risk adolescents, analyzed Census Bureau data, and conducted site visits in three urban neighborhoods: Ward 7 in Washington, DC; Boyle Heights in Los Angeles, California; and West Oakland, California, and a community redevelopment project in Detroit, Michigan. The researchers interviewed local officials, service providers, and teenage girls served by the social service providers.
Relevant findings	• Past prevention programs have shown little success in preventing first pregnancies or additional pregnancies among at-risk teenagers. Intervening after teenagers have become sexually active or have given birth is too late for positive impacts. The Office of Technology Assessment reviewed pregnancy prevention programs and found that no evidence existed of significantly reduced pregnancy rates among teenage girls. • Poverty, substance abuse, physical and sexual abuse, and neglect left teenage girls isolated and vulnerable. Most of these girls lived in households with incomes below the poverty level, with single parents who could offer little supervision, with high rates of parental substance abuse, and widespread physical and sexual abuse. In West Oakland, an Adolescent Family Life director believed that as many as 65 percent of the young girls served in her office had

been sexually abused. Community providers also reported that young girls are often unsupervised and have to assume adult responsibilities, including caring for young siblings.

- **Teenage girls in these neighborhoods feared for their safety and saw few places of refuge.** In Boyle Heights, gang violence was a serious problem, and an estimated 60 percent of the teenage girls were already in gang-related activities. Many girls said that they feared leaving their homes.

- **Teenage girls in these neighborhoods were at risk for multiple problems.** Research has found a correlation between adverse living conditions and poor outcomes. There are clear relationships between poverty and early, out-of-wedlock births. These young women were less likely to have completed their high school education. Their children had poorer overall health, putting them at risk of poor school performance. Parental drug abuse significantly increased the odds that an adolescent would become a substance abuser, and research showed that a woman's being abused as a child had an effect on her becoming a teenage mother.

- **At-risk teenage girls could be better served if approaches included early identification and treatment, long-term program commitment, and greater community involvement.** Services were offered to these girls only when problems reached a crisis state. For example, schools in all three communities in the study had special programs for teenagers who were either pregnant or already parents of young children. Few preventive services were in place, however, such as strategies to help teenagers avoid early sexual activity and pregnancy, resist drug use, avoid gang membership, and stay in school. In the Boyle Heights neighborhood, researchers found only one prevention program for teenage girls—Education Now and Babies Later. Many programs opened and then closed as funding disappeared; often, programs were begun in elementary school and then discontinued in middle or high school.

- **Few services were offered to help dysfunctional families.** In the neighborhoods visited, the number and scope of mental health and substance abuse services, and the number and scope of services to identify and prevent physical and sexual abuse and neglect, fell far short of the communities' needs. Providers believed that family dysfunction adversely affected the growth and development of young girls and could increase the likelihood of long-term dependency on public assistance. Providers reported that most parents were unprepared for their role as parents, unaware of or uninvolved in their children's activities, and often in need of clinical treatment themselves. Counselors from a West Oakland school estimated that 75 percent of mothers were insufficiently supportive of their children. Providers believed that this lack of attention and support for children was a function of long-standing patterns of parenting and a general sense of hopelessness in the community.

- **New service approaches depended on increased community leadership and involvement.** In Ward 7, West Oakland, and Detroit, coalitions and networks of local service providers were being developed to improve the capacity to address community needs. In Detroit, a comprehensive 20-year planning and coordination effort was developed jointly by the Kellogg Foundation, local providers, and residents. In Washington, the Teen Life Choices program established monthly lunch meetings that brought together many of the youth service providers in the community.

- **Local providers led efforts to build coalitions with area schools as a strategy to deliver coordinated programs to those individuals and families who need them.** In West Oakland, a middle school provided on-site case management and support services for students and their families, including individual and family counseling, home visits, crisis intervention, and community service referrals. A middle school principal was planning a program that would operate between 4 p.m. and 10 p.m., providing a fitness lab, computer/job skills training, medical information, mental health services, and parenting courses. Studies in West Oakland found that school-based programs reduced the number of discipline hearings and the number of suspensions for students in schools receiving services. In Detroit, a teenage health clinic within a middle school reported a reduction in teenage pregnancies from 14 in 1991 to 1 in 1993 and improved Scholastic Aptitude Test (SAT) scores over two years in both reading and mathematics. These communities also said that a school-based program's success depended on the support of the school's principal.

- **More comprehensive, integrated services are needed to address the problems of at-risk teenagers and their families.** The Urban Institute's review of programs serving at-risk teenagers included early identification and intervention; long-term and consistent intervention; individualized attention; emphasis on skills enhancement and life options; and development of multiple channels of influence, including parents, churches, and community organizations. Techniques that could integrate services include co-locating multiple service providers, joint planning among providers, and new local-level funding strategies. Necessary system changes include reorganization of administrative structures around common populations or problems, use of more flexible funding approaches, and creation of coordinated service planning at different levels of government.

GLOSSARY

AFDC—Aid to Families with Dependent Children
Aid to Dependent Children (ADC), established by the Social Security Act of 1935, was a cash grant program enabling states to assist children who had no fathers and were in need. It was renamed Aid to Families with Dependent Children (AFDC) in 1965. This program provides public assistance for children in need and their mothers or other caregiver relatives in all 50 states, the District of Columbia, Guam, Puerto Rico, and the Virgin Islands. Children are eligible if they have been deprived of parental support or care because their single mother or father is either continuously absent from home, incapacitated, unemployed, or deceased. In addition, some jurisdictions provide federal cash supplements to two-parent households in which one parent's unemployment creates such a need. Eligibility for this AFDC–Unemployed Parent (AFDC-UP) program is based on the unemployment status of the principal wage earner only. Each state defines "need," sets its own benefit levels, establishes income and resource limits within federal guidelines, and administers and supervises program administration.

Child Care Disregard
Federal law requires states to disregard certain earned income that went toward child care expenses when determining a family's AFDC or Food Stamps benefit level. The maximum amount that can be disregarded for child care is $175 per month per child ($200 for children under age 2).

CPS
The Current Population Survey is a continuing sampling study based on monthly interviews with about 57,000 U.S. households. The survey provides demographic and socioeconomic data on the population as a whole, the general labor force, and various subgroups of the population. Recent supplements cover subjects such as school enrollment, child support and alimony, fertility and birth rates, and child immunization status. The U.S. Bureau of Labor Statistics issues monthly bulletins, including *Monthly Labor Review and Employment and Earnings*.

DCTC
The Dependent Care Tax Credit provides a nonrefundable tax credit for up to 30 percent of employment-related dependent care expenses incurred to enable a taxpayer to work or look for work. Expenses are limited to $2,400 for one dependent individual and $4,800 for two or more. The credit applies to expenses for a child under 13 years of age, or a physically or mentally incapacitated family member.

EITC
The Earned Income Tax Credit is a refundable tax credit available to low-income workers. If the amount of the credit exceeds tax liability, the excess is payable directly to the taxpayer. The maximum credit a family can receive is $3,560 for those with incomes between $8,900 and $11,620. The credit phases out at $28,525 for families with more than one child.

FSA—Family Support Act of 1988
This federal welfare reform legislation changed the AFDC and Child Support Enforcement programs. The FSA created a program of education, training, and other work-related services for AFDC recipients and mandated the AFDC-UP program (AFDC for two-parent families) in all states. It strengthened the Child Support Enforcement program requirements for automatic wage withholding of child support, use of state child support guidelines, and the establishment of paternity. In addition, for families leaving AFDC because of increased earnings or loss of the earnings "disregards," the act extended Medicaid coverage to 12 months and established transitional child care assistance (see TCC below) for 12 months.

GA
General Assistance is a state-funded cash assistance program that provides benefits to non-elderly impoverished adults without dependent children. Of the 30 states that have GA programs, 17 made cuts in 1991–1992.

GED—High School general equivalency diploma

HSB
High School and Beyond is a survey that includes information collected from school administrators, teachers, parents, and high school sophomores and seniors in 1972, 1980, 1982, 1984, and 1986. Schools were grouped by type, with an over sampling of alternative, Hispanic, high-performance private, other non-Catholic private, and black Catholic schools. The purpose of HSB was to study students' transition from secondary school to early adulthood, i.e. post-high school education, employment, marriage, and family formation. Data were gathered on student coursework; academic performance; plans and aspirations for college; the influence of peers, parents, and teachers on educational goals; school-related activities; student attitudes toward school; personality characteristics; politics and social attitudes; family environment; and social and demographic background characteristics. The study was sponsored by the National Center for Education Statistics, U.S. Department of Education.

IHDP
The Infant Health and Development Program project was implemented during the mid-1980s with support from multiple public and foundation resources. The study's subjects were 985 low birthweight or premature infants from eight medical institutions. The infants received medical, developmental, and social assessments, home visits, and educationally-based day care at a child development center. Their parents participated in parent education programs and attended parent group meetings. The purpose of the program was to test the efficacy of combining early child development and family support services with pediatric surveillance to reduce the incidence of health and developmental problems among low birthweight premature infants. Secondary analyses of the data are being conducted, and follow-up assessments of children's cognitive, behavioral, and social competence at age five were recently completed.

JOBS—Job Opportunities and Basic Skills Training Program
This is a program under the Family Support Act (FSA) of 1988 whereby each state is required to educate, train, and employ welfare families. This program replaced the Work Incentive (WIN) program and consolidated other welfare-to-work provisions, such as the Job Training Partnership Act (JTPA). The FSA mandates that AFDC parents with children ages three and older must participate in JOBS or approved employment and training activities. Parents with children under six are required to participate for 20 hours per week.

MCHSBG
The Maternal and Child Health Services Block Grant is a federal block grant program, authorized under Title V of the Social Security Act. It provides funds to states for health services to pregnant women, infants, children, and adolescents. States determine which services they provide, which can include prenatal care, well-child clinics, immunizations, dental care, family planning, and a wide range of inpatient and outpatient services for children with special health care needs.

NHIS–CHS
The National Health Interview Survey, Child Health Supplement was designed and funded by the National Center for Health Statistics to provide more detailed information on the physical and mental health, school performance, and behavior of children than available from the NHIS core survey. Information was gathered on one child for each participating family in the survey. Altogether, 15,416 children were included in the 1981 Supplement and 17,110 in the 1988 Supplement. Information collected included: child care arrangements; contact with biological parents living outside the household; the biological mother's marital history; residential mobility; motor and social development; prenatal care; health conditions; hospitalizations and surgery; height and weight; sleep habits; use of medications; progress and behavior in school; and psychological problems and counseling. Data from the Survey are published by the National Center for Health Statistics in *Vital and Health Statistics*, Series 10.

NLSY
The National Longitudinal Survey of Youth is part of a series of surveys exploring the labor market experiences of several population groups facing employment problems of particular concern to policymakers. The sample is approximately 5,800 females and an equal number of males, ages 14–21. Blacks, Hispanics, and disadvantaged youth are all oversampled to facilitate analysis of youth in these groups. Questions focus on the school-to-work transition; occupational choice; earnings; adaptation to the world of work; and work-family issues. Questions on drug and alcohol use, illegal activities or employment, family planning, child care, and maternal and child health care are also included. The survey is sponsored by the U.S. Department of Labor, with additional support from several of the National Institutes of Health and from the Department of Defense.

NSFH
The National Survey of Families and Households is a national cross-sectional survey with over 13,000 respondents. It was funded by the Center for Population Research of the National Institute of Child Health and Human Development. The survey was conducted by the University of Wisconsin from 1987 to 1989. Survey questions focused on changes in U.S. patterns of fertility, marriage, mortality, migration, family composition and household structure. In addition to demographic information, questions were included on psychological well-being; satisfaction with work, marriage, and parenthood; alcohol and drug abuse; health; and access to and receipt of social services.

PSID
The Panel Study of Income Dynamics is an ongoing study sponsored by the National Science Foundation, with supplemental funding from several public and foundation sources. The study is based on yearly telephone interviews with about 5,000 families, with an over sampling of low-income and minority households. The PSID collects information on changes in the economic well-being of families, to explore whether any public policy changes would make a difference in improving their lives. The study follows a sample over time to gain insight into the demographic, economic, behavioral, and attitudinal variables that affect a family's economic well-being.

RCBP
The Revised Child Behavior Profile is a 120-item questionnaire that measures behavioral functioning in children ages 4 and 5. Mothers characterize statements about their child's behavior in the past six months. Higher scores indicate more behavior problems.

SIPP
The Survey of Income and Program Participation is a major source of information on the demographic and economic status of individuals and families in the U.S. The survey provides a better understanding of the distribution of wealth, income, and poverty, and of the effects of federal and state programs on the well-being of individuals and families in the U.S. Participating households (over 11,500 in 1986) are interviewed once every four months for a period of two and a half years. Individuals are followed even if they change their address or move out of the household. The survey collects information on demographic characteristics, labor force participation, earnings and income, tax data, disability and work history, migration, fertility, child care, child support, health information, and public assistance recipiency. The U.S. Bureau of the Census funds and conducts the survey.

SSI
Supplemental Security Income is a means-tested, federally administered income assistance program authorized by Title XVI of the Social Security Act. It provides monthly cash payments to needy, aged, blind, and disabled persons in accordance with national income and eligibility standards. The program was expanded to include children after a court case in 1990 concluded that a child with impairments of comparable severity to that of an adult may be considered disabled. In 1994, the SSI monthly benefit standard was $446 for an individual and $669 for a couple.

TCC
The Transitional Child Care Assistance program is a federal, AFDC-linked child care subsidy program that requires states to guarantee up to 12 months of child care to a family who loses AFDC eligibility due to reasons related to employment. To be eligible for TCC, families must have received AFDC in at least three of the last six months before becoming ineligible for AFDC benefits. Families contribute to the cost of care based on a state-established sliding fee scale.

WIC
The Special Supplemental Food Program for Women, Infants and Children provides nutritional screening and food assistance to low-income pregnant and postpartum women and their infants and children up to age five. Participants in the program must have incomes at or below 185 percent of the federal poverty line, and must be nutritionally at risk.

WPPSI
Wechsler Preschool and Primary Scale of Intelligence is a test of cognitive functioning that was developed for use with children ages 4 to 6 1/2 years. Higher scores on the WPPSI indicate higher IQ levels.

**NATIONAL CENTER
FOR CHILDREN IN POVERTY**
COLUMBIA UNIVERSITY SCHOOL OF PUBLIC HEALTH

154 Haven Avenue, New York, NY 10032
Tel: (212) 927-8793   Fax (212) 927-9162
WWW: http://cpmcnet.columbia.edu/dept/nccp/

OAKLAND COMMUNITY COLLEGE

3 2355 00245670 5

Oakland Community College
Orchard Ridge Campus Library
27055 Orchard Lake Road
Farmington Hills, MI 48334

HV 699 .C65 1996
Collins, Ann.
Children and welfare reform

occOR Sep-09-1998 16:50

DATE DUE			
NOV 01 2005			
DEC 19 2011			

**OAKLAND COMMUNITY COLLEGE
ORCHARD RIDGE LIBRARY**
27055 ORCHARD LAKE ROAD
FARMINGTON HILLS, MI 48334

DEMCO